CONTENT

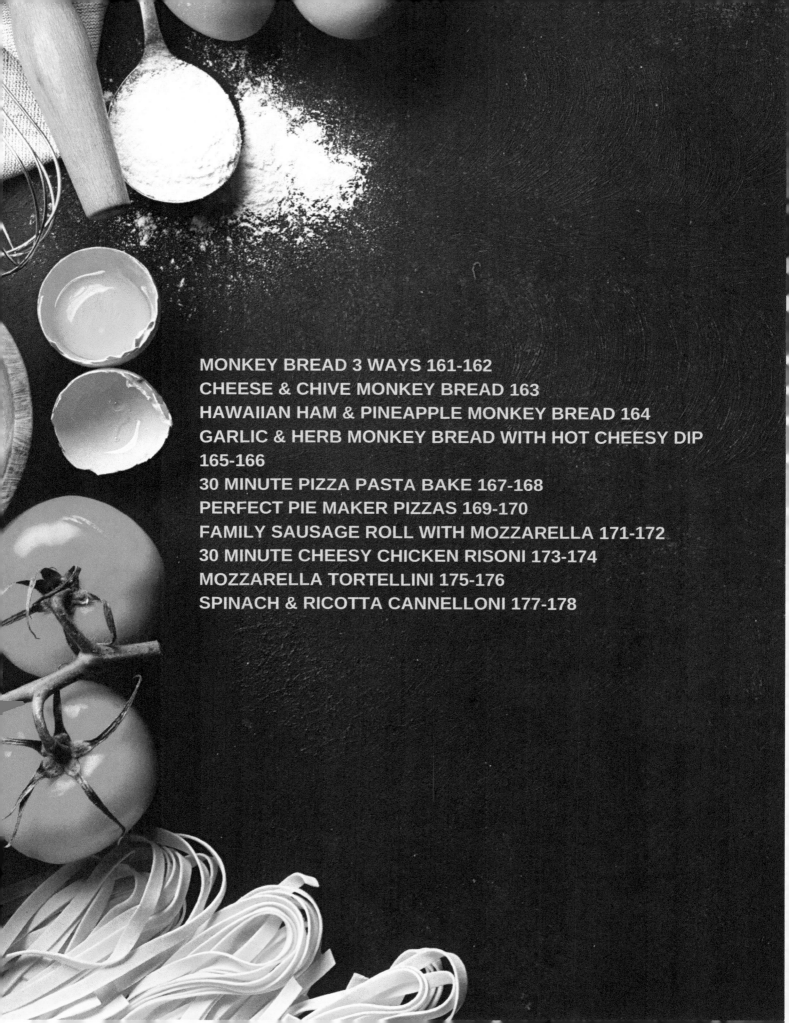

Tip

Sneak chopped carrots into the mince mixture for an extra veggie hit

LASAGNE *roll-ups*

 PREP 20 MINS   **COOK** 50 MINS **MAKES** 16

INGREDIENTS

⅓ cup olive oil

500g beef mince

1 brown onion, finely diced

2 x 400g can Ardmona Diced
Tomatoes

3 garlic cloves, crushed

2 tbs Italian seasoning

8 fresh lasagne sheets, cut in half,
lengthways

Salt and pepper

RICOTTA FILLING

500g ricotta

1 egg, whisked

⅓ cup flat leaf parsley, chopped,
plus extra to serve

3 ½ cups three cheese blend

METHOD

1. Preheat oven to 180°C

2. Heat 1 tablespoon of oil in a large non-stick frying
   pan over medium high heat. Cook mince, breaking
   up with a wooden spoon. Add the onion and cook,
   stirring until meat is brown and onions are soft

3. Add 1 can of tomatoes, the garlic and Italian
   seasoning. Stir the sauce over low heat, then
   simmer, covered, for 10 minutes

4. Meanwhile, make the Ricotta Filling

5. Before assembling the roll-ups, evenly spread
   remaining can of tomatoes over the base of a
   6-cup ovenproof baking dish

6. Prepare the pasta by placing the lasagne sheets
   in a single layer on a lined baking tray

7. Spread ¼ cup of Ricotta Filling over each of the
   lasagne sheets. Then spread a heaped tablespoon
   of the meat sauce on top

8. Roll up each filled lasagne sheet and arrange in the
   baking dish standing upright, nestling them together

9. Cover with any remaining meat sauce and sprinkle
   remaining cheese over. Carefully tent an extra long
   piece of aluminium foil to cover the bake, ensuring
   it does not touch the cheese. Bake for 30 minutes or
   until pasta is cooked. Remove foil and bake for
   a further 5 minutes to allow lasagne to turn golden
   and slightly crisp

RICOTTA FILLING

1. Put ricotta, egg, parsley, salt and pepper in a
   medium bowl. Add 3 cups of the cheese mix
   and stir to combine

Tip

Very finely chop the mushrooms to get them past fussy eaters

MUSHROOM
spaghetti bolognese

 PREP 15 MINS   **COOK** 45 MINS **SERVES** 4

INGREDIENTS

2 tbs olive oil

1 brown onion, finely chopped

2 garlic cloves, crushed

2 tbs tomato paste

400g pork mince (see tip)

400g Button Mushrooms, sliced

2 tsp thyme leaves

800g can chopped tomatoes

400g spaghetti

¼ cup shredded basil leaves, plus extra whole leaves, to serve

Finely grated parmesan, to serve

METHOD

1. Heat olive oil in a large saucepan over medium heat. Add onion and garlic and cook, stirring, 5 minutes or until onion softens. Add tomato paste and cook for 1 minute

2. Add mince, increase heat to medium-high and cook, stirring, for 3-4 minutes or until browned all over. Add mushrooms and thyme and cook for a further 3 minutes

3. Add tomatoes, bring to a simmer. Season to taste. Reduce heat to low, and simmer for 30 minutes or until the sauce thickens

4. Cook spaghetti in a saucepan of boiling salted water following packet instructions. Drain and set aside

5. Add drained pasta and shredded basil to the sauce, mix well. Divide pasta between serving bowls. Serve topped with parmesan and extra basil

TIPS & HINTS:

Bolognese can be made with any variety of mince, shop smart and check out the best buy of the week

Top tip

For a delicious veg only option, leave out the chicken

OVEN-BAKED CHICKEN
& mushroom risotto

 PREP 15 MINS   **COOK** 45 MINS   **SERVES** 4

INGREDIENTS

2 tbs olive oil

500g chicken thigh fillets, cut into 3cm pieces

1 brown onion, finely diced

3 garlic cloves, finely chopped

250g Swiss Brown Mushrooms, sliced

2 cups arborio rice

4 cups (1L) chicken stock

50g baby spinach leaves

½ cup grated parmesan

Lemon wedges, to serve

METHOD

1. Preheat oven to 160°C fan-forced. Heat 1 tbs oil in a large ovenproof pan over medium-high heat. Brown chicken in 2 batches. Transfer to a plate. Set aside

2. Heat remaining 1 tbs oil in the pan over medium heat. Add onion and garlic. Cook, stirring often, for 3-4 minutes or until onion softens. Toss through mushrooms. Cook for 1 minute

3. Stir in rice. Cook, stirring, for 1-2 minutes or until rice is glossy. Add stock and return chicken to pan. Stir to combine and bring to the boil. Cover and bake for 25-30 minutes or until rice is just tender and liquid has almost been absorbed. Toss through spinach. Sprinkle with parmesan. Serve with lemon wedges

SALAMI TOMATO
& ricotta pizzas

 PREP 10 MINS **COOK** 10 MINS 👤 **SERVES** 4

Recipe uses products from brands supporting **Foodbank**

INGREDIENTS

2 large Lebanese flatbreads

4 tbs tomato paste

2 x 80g packet Primo Thinly Sliced Danish Salami

100g grape or cherry tomatoes, halved

100g fresh ricotta, crumbled

Olive oil cooking spray

Rocket leaves & extra virgin olive oil, to serve

METHOD

1. Preheat oven to 200°C fan-forced. Place the flatbreads onto baking trays. Spread each with 2 tbs tomato paste

2. Dividing ingredients, top each with salami, tomato and sprinkle with ricotta. Spray with oil

3. Bake for 10 minutes or until bread is crisp. Scatter with rocket. Season. Drizzle with extra virgin olive oil and serve

{ *You can also use pre-made pizza bases available from most major supermakets* }

CHICKEN FETTUCCINE WITH CREAMY
avocado pasta sauce

 PREP 15 MINS **COOK** 15 MINS 🧍 **SERVES** 4

INGREDIENTS

500g chicken breast fillets

2 garlic cloves

2 Avocados

½ bunch basil, leaves picked, roughly chopped

½ cup finely grated parmesan

1 lemon, finely grated rind and juice

¼ cup olive oil, plus extra to drizzle

Sea salt flakes and white pepper

500g cherry truss tomatoes

400g fettuccine pasta

Finely grated or shaved parmesan, to serve

⅓ cup small basil leaves, to serve

METHOD

1. Place chicken into a deep frying pan and cover with cold water. Place over a medium heat and bring to a simmer. Cook for 10 minutes. Remove from heat and cool in water. Drain chicken and shred

2. Meanwhile, place garlic, avocados, basil, parmesan, lemon rind and juice and olive oil into a food processor. Season and puree until a smooth green sauce forms

3. Preheat oven to 180°C. Line a baking tray with baking paper. Place tomatoes onto tray and drizzle with oil. Season with salt and pepper. Roast for 15 minutes or until softened

4. Cook pasta in a large saucepan of salted boiling water until just tender as per packet instructions. Drain and return to saucepan. Add shredded chicken and avocado sauce to pasta. Toss until well combined. Serve pasta topped with parmesan, basil leaves and roasted tomatoes

Twist

We've given
the Italian-Aussie
parmigiana an
avolicious update!

EASY AVOCADO *parmigiana*

PREP 10 MINS **COOK** 15 MINS **SERVES** 4

INGREDIENTS

4 chicken breast fillets

⅓ cup plain flour

2 eggs, lightly whisked

1 cup Panko breadcrumbs

Olive oil, for shallow frying

2 tbs Dijon mustard

1 just-ripe Avocado, skin and seed removed, sliced

4 slices Swiss cheese

METHOD

1. Preheat oven to 200°C/180°C fan-forced. Grease and line a baking tray with baking paper
2. Place 1 chicken breast between 2 sheets of baking paper. Gently flatten with a rolling pin to ½cm thick. Repeat with remaining chicken
3. Coat each chicken breast in flour, shaking off the excess. Dip in egg, and press into breadcrumbs, coating both sides
4. Add enough oil to a non-stick frying pan to shallow fry. Heat the oil then add the chicken and fry for about 2 minutes on each side or until golden
5. Transfer to prepared tray. Evenly spread mustard over the top side of the chicken. Top with sliced avocado and then the cheese
6. Bake for 7-8 minutes or until cheese has melted and chicken is cooked through
7. Remove from oven and serve with a simple salad

CHICKEN SATAY SKEWERS
with gado gado

 PREP 15 MINS + MARINATING TIME **COOK** 20 MINS **SERVES** 4

INGREDIENTS

750g chicken thigh fillets, cut into 4cm cubes

200g Passage to Asia Satay Chicken stir-fry sauce

150g green beans, trimmed

3 cups finely shredded Savoy cabbage

1 carrot, finely shredded

1 Lebanese cucumber, thinly sliced diagonally

1 small red onion, thinly sliced

4 eggs, hard boiled, halved

Roasted peanuts, chopped, to serve

METHOD

1. Place chicken into a bowl and add Passage to Asia Satay Chicken stir-fry sauce, reserving ¼ cup to serve. Stir until well combined. Cover and marinate for 30 minutes. Thread diced chicken onto the soaked skewers

2. Meanwhile, bring a medium saucepan of water to the boil. Fill a large bowl with iced water. Cook beans for 2 minutes or until just tender. Transfer to iced water. Add cabbage to boiling water and cook for 2 minutes or until wilted. Add carrot and cook for 1 minute or until wilted. Transfer to bowl with beans.

3. Preheat oven to 180°C. Drain vegetables and place with cucumber, onion and egg onto a large platter

4. Heat a chargrill over high heat or large non-stick frying pan over medium-high heat. Line a baking tray with baking paper. Chargrill skewers for 8 minutes or until browned on all sides. Transfer to tray. Place in oven for 10 minutes or until cook through. Serve skewers with gado gado, reserved sauce, chopped peanuts

TIPS & HINTS:
You will need to pre-soak 12 small wooden skewers

TERIYAKI BEEF
noodles

 PREP 10 MINS **COOK** 20 MINS **SERVES** 4

INGREDIENTS

2 tbs vegetable oil

500g rump steak, cut into thin strips

1 carrot, halved lengthways, thinly sliced diagonally

1 red capsicum, deseeded, thinly sliced

1 bunch broccolini, trimmed, halved lengthways, cut into thirds

100g snow peas, trimmed, halved lengthways diagonally

4 green onions, thinly sliced diagonally

200g Passage to Asia Teriyaki Chicken stir-fry sauce

450g pkt hokkien noodles, cooked, drained

Toasted sesame seeds, to serve

Extra thinly sliced green onions, to serve

METHOD

1. Heat 2 tsp oil in a wok over a high heat. Cook steak in batches, for 2 minutes or until browned, adding more oil as required. Transfer to a bowl

2. Add carrot and capsicum to wok and stir-fry for 2 minutes. Add broccolini and snow peas and toss until combined. Add 2 tbs water and cook for 2 minutes or until vegetables are just softened. Return steak to wok with green onion and Passage to Asia Teriyaki Chicken stir-fry sauce. Stir until combined. Cook for 2 minutes or until heated through. Add noodles and toss to combine. Serve topped with sesame seeds and extra green onion

Tip

Add steamed rice for a more substantial meal

KATSU PORK
WITH PEAR
& carrot slaw

 PREP 20 MINS   **COOK** 20 MINS 👤 **SERVES** 4

INGREDIENTS

3 firm pears, quartered, cored

1 carrot

2 green onions, thinly sliced diagonally

2 tbs pickled pink ginger, chopped

¼ cup mayonnaise

1 lime, juiced

4 heart-smart pork loin medallions

⅓ cup plain flour

1 egg

1 cup panko breadcrumbs

2 tbs vegetable oil

20g butter

200g Passage to Asia Japanese Katsu Curry Sauce

METHOD

1. Coarsely grate pear and carrot and place in a bowl. Add onion, ginger, mayonnaise, lime juice, salt and white pepper and stir until well combined. Cover and refrigerate until required

2. Place your hand flat over a pork loin and using a sharp knife, cut through the centre from one side to the other. When almost at the other side, open pork loin out forming a thin schnitzel. Repeat with remaining pork loins

3. Place flour into a shallow bowl. Whisk egg in a shallow bowl with 1 tbs of water and place breadcrumbs into another bowl. Lightly coat schnitzels with flour, then coat with egg and breadcrumbs

4. Heat oil and butter in a large frying pan over medium heat. Cook schnitzels for 3 minutes each side or until golden and cooked through. Place Passage to Asia Japanese Katsu Curry Sauce into a small saucepan and place over a medium heat. Cook for 4 minutes or until hot. Serve schnitzel sliced and sauce spooned over with pear and carrot slaw on the side

TIPS & HINTS:

We used Kewpie mayonnaise

CHICKEN & PRAWN
pad Thai

 PREP 20 MINS **COOK** 20 MINS **SERVES** 4

INGREDIENTS

375g pad Thai rice noodles

2 tbs vegetable oil

16 green prawns, peeled, deveined

500g chicken thigh fillets, diced

2 eggs, whisked

5 green onions, thinly sliced diagonally

225g Passage to Asia Pad Thai stir-fry sauce

1 cup bean sprouts, trimmed

Small red chillies, thinly sliced, to serve

Thai basil, to serve

METHOD

1. Cook rice noodles as per packet instructions.

2. Heat 1 tbs oil in a hot wok. Add prawns and cook for 3 minutes or until just cooked. Transfer to a bowl. Add chicken and cook for 5 minutes or until browned and cooked through. Transfer to bowl with prawns.

3. Heat remaining oil. Add egg and cook for 1 minute or until just set. Add onion and stir until combined. Return chicken, prawns and noodles to wok with Passage to Asia Pad Thai stir-fry sauce. Toss until well combined and heated through. Remove from heat and stir in bean sprouts. Spoon into serving bowls and top with chilli and basil.

SPICED SPATCHCOCK
with citrus couscous

 PREP 15 MINS (PLUS MARINATING TIME)   **COOK** 35 MINS   **SERVES** 4

INGREDIENTS

SPICE MIX

½ red onion, roughly chopped

1 clove crushed garlic

1 tsp turmeric

2 tsp ground cumin

2 tsp paprika

¼ tsp each cayenne, sea salt
and freshly ground black pepper

1 tbs fresh coriander leaves

2 tbs parsley leaves

2 tbs olive oil

4 spatchcock, backbone removed
and halved

CITRUS COUSCOUS SALAD

1 cup instant couscous

1 cup boiling water

2 tbs extra virgin olive oil

1 small red capsicum, diced

2 tbs each of orange and lemon juice

1 tbs preserved lemon rind, finely
chopped

2 tbs shredded mint

½ tsp each cinnamon and nutmeg

Greek yoghurt and extra coriander
(optional), to serve

METHOD

SPICE MIX

1. To make the spice mix, pound all ingredients in a mortar and pestle or process until well blended

2. Coat the spatchcock with spice mix and refrigerate for a few hours so that the flavours can develop

3. Heat the barbecue to medium and oil the bars to prevent the spatchcock from sticking. Place the spatchcocks on the grill, skin-side down, and cook for about 10 minutes each side or until juices run clear when the thigh is pierced with a sharp knife. Cover with foil and set aside for a few minutes to rest

CITRUS COUSCOUS SALAD

1. Place couscous in a large bowl, pour over boiling water, cover with plastic wrap and set aside for 5 minutes. Fluff up the grains with a fork then set aside for a further 5 minutes

2. Fluff again to break up any lumps. Stir together olive oil, capsicum, juices, preserved lemon, mint, cinnamon and nutmeg and pour over the couscous, toss to combine

3. Pile couscous onto plates or platter, top with spatchcock and serve with yoghurt. Garnish with extra coriander if you like.

AVOCADO
hummus

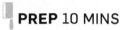

INGREDIENTS

400g can chickpeas, drained and rinsed

2 small garlic cloves, peeled

¼ cup firmly-packed coriander leaves

¼ cup extra virgin olive oil

2 tbs lime juice

1 tbs tahini

½ tsp ground cumin

2 ripe Avocados, seeds and skin removed, chopped

1 tbs water

Toasted pita bread, to serve

METHOD

1. In a food processor, blend chickpeas, garlic, coriander, oil and lime juice until smooth

2. Add tahini, cumin and avocados. Process again until combined, adding water if necessary for desired consistency. Season to taste

3. Serve with extra scattered chickpeas and toasted pita bread

{ *Top with smoked paprika to give it extra spice and a smoky flavour* }

Tip

Add shredded
roast chicken for
a hearty dinner

WARM MOROCCAN AVOCADO & ROASTED
vegetable salad

 PREP 20 MINS   **COOK** 30 MINS   **SERVES** 4

INGREDIENTS

ROASTED VEGETABLE SALAD

2 tbs olive oil

1 tsp ground cumin

1 tsp ground coriander

2 garlic cloves, crushed

750g orange sweet potato, peeled and cut into bite-sized pieces

400g (about 2 bunches) baby Dutch carrots, trimmed and peeled

MOROCCAN AVOCADO

2 just-ripe Avocados, halved and deseeded

100g feta cheese, crumbled

1 tbs lemon juice

2 tsp dukkah

50g baby spinach leaves

½ pomegranate, seeds removed

Lemon wedges and warmed flatbread, to serve

METHOD

ROASTED VEGETABLE SALAD

1. Preheat oven to 200°C/180°C fan-forced

2. Combine oil, cumin, coriander and garlic in a bowl

3. Arrange sweet potatoes and carrots in a single layer on a large baking tray lined with baking paper. Drizzle with oil mixture and toss to coat vegetables

4. Roast vegetables, turning once, for 25-30 minutes or until tender

MOROCCAN AVOCADO

1. Meanwhile scoop the avocado flesh into a bowl and add feta, lemon juice and sprinkle with dukkah. Gently toss to combine and set aside until the vegetables are cooked

2. To serve, arrange roasted vegetables and spinach on a serving platter. Top with avocado mixture and sprinkle with pomegranate seeds. Season to taste

3. Serve with lemon wedges and flatbread

MIDDLE EASTERN QUAIL & COUSCOUS SALAD WITH

garlic sauce

PREP 20 MINS (PLUS MARINATING TIME) **COOK** 20 MINS **SERVES** 4

INGREDIENTS

GARLIC SAUCE

1 egg yolk

5 garlic cloves, crushed

Pinch salt

1 tbs lemon juice

100ml vegetable oil

CORIANDER SALT

2 tbs coriander seeds

1 tsp cumin seeds

1 tbs sea salt

QUAIL & COUSCOUS SALAD

400g Quail Breast Fillets

1 cup couscous

1 cup boiling water

1 Lebanese cucumber, seeds removed and diced

2 roma tomatoes, diced

½ small red onion, diced

1 x 400g can chickpeas, rinsed and drained

½ cup chopped coriander leaves

2 tbs lemon juice

2 tbs olive oil, extra for brushing

METHOD

GARLIC SAUCE

1. Place egg yolk, garlic, salt and lemon into a food processor and pulse. With the food processor running, add oil in a slow steady stream until a mayonnaise forms. Set aside

CORIANDER SALT

1. Place spices into a dry frying pan and heat over a low heat, shaking pan, until just fragrant. Add salt and heat a further 1–2 minutes. Transfer to a plate to cool completely. Grind to a fine powder in a mortar and pestle or spice grinder

QUAIL & COUSCOUS SALAD

1. Rub coriander salt into quail to cover evenly and refrigerate, uncovered, for at least 1 hour

2. Place couscous into a bowl and pour over boiling water; stand for 5 minutes. Fluff couscous with a fork to separate grains. Stir through chopped vegetables, chickpeas and herbs and mix well. Whisk lemon juice and oil together and season. Stir through salad

3. Heat a chargrill or barbecue plate over medium-high heat; brush quail skin with oil and cook Breast Fillets for 3 minutes each side or until cooked to your liking

4. To serve, spoon couscous salad onto plates, top with quail and a dollop of the garlic sauce

Top Tip

Halve the amount
of chilli powder for
a milder option

MEXICAN
spatchcock

 PREP 15 MINS  **COOK** 10 MINS   **SERVES** 2

INGREDIENTS

MEXICAN SPATCHCOCK

1 pack Game Farm deboned spatchcock (300 - 350g)

1 tsp chilli powder

½ tsp dried oregano

⅛ tsp ground cinnamon

1 garlic clove, crushed

2 tbs lemon juice

SALSA

Chargrilled corn kernels

1 tomato, diced

1 small red onion, sliced

1 red chilli, finely chopped

Coriander leaves

Lime juice

TO SERVE

Tortillas

Guacamole

Shredded Lettuce

METHOD

MEXICAN SPATCHCOCK

1. Thread each spatchcock onto a skewer

2. Combine the spices, garlic and lemon juice and brush generously over the spatchcock

3. Heat a grillpan or frypan over medium heat and cook the spatchcock for 5 minutes on each side or until cooked through

SALSA

1. Combine salsa ingredients

TO SERVE

1. Serve the spatchcock with salsa, tortilla, lettuce and guacamole

FANTASTIC FISH
tortillas

 PREP 10 MINS **COOK** 15 MINS  **SERVES** 4

Recipe uses products from brands supporting **Foodbank**

INGREDIENTS

CHIPOTLE LIME CREAM

2 tbs chipotle sauce

½ cup aioli

1 lime, halved

COLESLAW

4 cups shredded red cabbage

3 shallots, thinly sliced

1 large carrot, shredded

FISH TORTILLAS

⅓ cup Flour

2 tbs Old El Paso™ Taco Spice Mix

600g firm white fish fillets, cut into 15cm pieces

Olive oil, for frying

1 packet Old El Paso™ Stand 'N Stuff™ Tortillas

Coriander, to serve

1 lime, halved

METHOD

CHIPOTLE LIME CREAM

1. To make the cream sauce, combine chipotle, aioli and lime juice in a medium sized bowl. Season and whisk until combined

COLESLAW

1. In a medium bowl, add coleslaw ingredients and mix to combine

FISH TORTILLAS

1. Mix the flour with the taco spice mix and use to coat the fish pieces

2. Heat oil in a non-stick frying pan over medium-high heat. Gently fry the fish in batches, cleaning the pan in between each batch and repeat until all fish is cooked. Keep warm

3. Serve tortillas filled with coleslaw, topped with fish, chipotle cream, extra coriander and a squeeze of lime

MEXICAN CHICKEN
& rice casserole

 **PREP** 10 MINS **COOK** 35 MINS  **SERVES** 8

Recipe uses products from brands supporting **Foodbank**

INGREDIENTS

1 ½ cups SunRice Medium Grain
White Rice

3 cups chicken stock

425g can mexibeans

3 cups shredded roast chicken

375g jar enchilada sauce

250g tub sour cream

4 shallots, thinly sliced, plus extra
for garnish

1½ cups cheese blend

METHOD

1. Preheat oven 180°C. Grease a 10 cup-capacity baking dish

2. Cook rice according to packet instructions, swapping the water for the chicken stock

3. In a medium bowl, combine cooked rice, chicken, beans, enchilada sauce, sour cream, shallots and 1 cup of the cheese. Pour into a baking dish. Cover with foil and bake for 20 minutes

4. Remove the foil and sprinkle over the remaining cheese. Return the casserole to the oven and bake for a further 5-10 minutes or until cheese is completely melted and golden

5. Top with extra shallots and serve immediately

TIPS & HINTS:

You can spice things up by adding some chopped jalapenos on top of the casserole after baking. We used Old El Paso™ Mexe-Beans and Old El Paso™ Enchilada Sauce and Devondale Three Cheese Blend in this recipe

tip

Change it up and
substitute chicken
with stir-fried
veggies

BAKED BEAN & CHICKEN
enchiladas

 PREP 25 MINS   **COOK** 25 MINS   **SERVES** 4

Recipe uses products from brands supporting **Foodbank**

INGREDIENTS

3 cups shredded roasted chicken

425g can SPC Baked Beans

2 cups Devondale Three
Cheese Blend

2 tbs Old El Paso™ Fajita Spice Mix

½ cup coriander, plus extra leaves
to serve

375g jar Old El Paso™ Mild Thick
'N Chunky Salsa

10 pack Old El Paso™
Regular Tortillas

Sour cream, to serve

METHOD

1. Preheat oven to 200°C. Grease and line an ovenproof
   baking dish

2. In a large bowl, combine chicken with baked beans,
   half the cheese, fajita spice mix, coriander and
   1½ cups salsa

3. Divide the mixture evenly down the centre of the
   tortillas (approx ⅓ cup). Roll up firmly to close and
   place seam-side down onto prepared baking dish.
   Repeat until all tortillas are filled

4. Spoon remaining salsa over the tortillas and scatter
   over remaining cheese

5. Bake in the oven for about 20 minutes or until cheese
   is melted and golden brown

6. Serve with sour cream and extra coriander leaves

LEMONADE
scones

PREP 10-12 MINS · **COOK** 15 MINS · **MAKES** 12 SLICES

INGREDIENTS

LEMONADE SCONES

3 cups self-raising flour

½ tsp baking powder

1 tsp sugar

60g Copha

300ml lemonade

*Plain flour, for kneading
and rolling*

1 egg, beaten

METHOD

1. Pre-heat oven to 190°C
2. In a large bowl, combine the self-raising flour, baking powder and sugar
3. Grate the Copha over the flour. Rub the Copha into the flour until mixture resembles fine breadcrumbs
4. Make a well in the centre of the flour mixture and pour in ¾ of the lemonade. Mix to a firm but tacky dough, adding more lemonade if required
5. Turn dough out onto a lightly floured board and knead gently
6. Roll dough out to a 4cm thick circle
7. Using a floured cutter, cut out scones. Re-roll dough as required
8. Place scones onto a floured non-stick baking tray. Brush scones with beaten egg and bake in the pre-heated oven at 190°C for 12-15 minutes
9. Cool on a wire rack and serve warm

TIPS & HINTS:

If making date or sultana scones, add ½ cup of fruit and 1 beaten egg to the mixture

ANZAC
biscuits

 **PREP** 15 MINS **COOK** 12 MINS **MAKES** 18 BISCUITS

INGREDIENTS

125g (½ block) Fairy margarine

3 tbs golden syrup

½ tsp bicarb soda

2 tbs hot water

150g (1 cup) plain flour, sifted

110g (½ cup) caster sugar

90g (1 cup) desiccated coconut

90g (1 cup) rolled oats

METHOD

1. Pre-heat oven to 150°C. Line 2 baking trays with baking paper

2. Melt Fairy and golden syrup in a small saucepan over low heat. Add the bicarb soda mixed with water

3. Combine the dry ingredients in a large mixing bowl, pour melted Fairy mixture into the centre and mix together

4. Roll heaped tablespoons of the mixture and place on the prepared trays. Flatten the mix down with the palm of your hand until approx. 1cm

5. Bake for 10–12 minutes or until golden brown. Cool on a cooling rack

Tip

Store in an airtight container for up to 3 days

ADD SULTANAS,
DRIED CRANBERRIES OR
CHOCOLATE CHIPS FOR
EXTRA GOODNESS

HONEY *joys*

 PREP 8-10 MINS   **COOK** 15 MINS   **MAKES** 18 HONEY JOYS

INGREDIENTS

60g Copha

2 tbs honey

⅓ cup sugar

4 cups corn flakes

METHOD

1. Pre-heat oven 150°C
2. Melt together the Copha, honey and sugar in a saucepan over low heat, stirring until the sugar has dissolved. Allow mixture to cool slightly
3. Place the corn flakes into a large mixing bowl, then pour the Copha mixture over. Mix well to coat flakes
4. Spoon the honey joy mixture into muffin trays lined with paper cases
5. Bake the honey joys in the pre-heated oven at 150°C for 10 minutes
6. Remove tray from oven and cool on a wire rack. Honey joys will firm on cooling
7. When cool, store in an airtight tin

TIPS:

These honey joys are gluten free

Tip

Mix up the flavour by using a different jam variety

MELTING
moments

 PREP 20 MINS   **COOK** 12 MINS   **MAKES** 10 BISCUITS

INGREDIENTS

BISCUITS

125g (½ block) Fairy margarine, softened

75g (½ cup) icing sugar, sifted

½ tsp vanilla essence

100g (⅔ cup) plain flour, sifted

75g (½ cup) cornflour, sifted

ORANGE CREAM

60g (¼ block) Fairy margarine, softened

160g (1 cup) icing sugar, sifted

1 tsp grated orange rind

½ tbs orange juice

ASSEMBLY

Raspberry jam, to serve

Icing sugar, to dust

METHOD

BISCUITS

1. Preheat oven to 160°C. Line baking trays with baking paper
2. Cream Fairy, icing sugar and vanilla together until light and fluffy. Add flour and cornflour and mix well
3. Roll heaped teaspoons of mixture into balls and place on the prepared trays. Flatten with the back of a fork to make an indent
4. Bake in oven for 10-12 mins until golden

ORANGE CREAM

1. Beat Fairy until smooth. Gradually add icing sugar. Beat until light and creamy
2. Add the rind and juice, and beat until combined

ASSEMBLY

1. Sandwich 2 biscuits together with the orange filling and some raspberry jam
2. Dust with icing sugar

For white chocolate crackles, substitute the cocoa powder with milk powder and add 200g white chocolate

45

CHOCOLATE
crackles

 PREP 10 MINS (PLUS SETTING TIME) **COOK** 5 MINS **MAKES** 12

INGREDIENTS

250g (1 block) Copha

125g (1 cup) icing sugar

60g (½ cup) cocoa powder

4 cups Rice Bubbles

100g (1 cup) desiccated coconut

METHOD

1. Line a standard 12 cup muffin tray with paper cases.
2. Melt Copha in microwave on high or in a saucepan until fully melted. Mix Rice Bubbles, icing sugar, cocoa powder and desiccated coconut in a large bowl. Add in the melted Copha, and stir to combine.
3. Spoon crackle mix evenly into the prepared muffin cups. Place in fridge for 1 hour to set.

CHOCOLATE CRACKLES AREN'T JUST FOR PARTIES, ADD TO LUNCH BOXES FOR A GLUTEN-FREE TREAT.

47

RASPBERRY
coconut slice

 PREP 10 MINS   **COOK** 20 MINS   **MAKES** 12 SLICES

INGREDIENTS

BASE

125g (½ block) Fairy margarine, softened

110g (½ cup) caster sugar

1 egg

225g (1½cups) self-raising flour, sifted

TOPPING

90g (1 cup) desiccated coconut

110g (½ cup) caster sugar

1 egg

½ tsp vanilla essence

2 tbs raspberry jam

METHOD

BASE

1. Preheat oven to 180°C. Line a 20cm square sandwich tin with baking paper
2. Cream Fairy and sugar together until light and fluffy. Beat in the egg and fold into the flour
3. Press the mixture into prepared tin

TOPPING

1. Combine coconut, sugar, egg and vanilla together, mix well
2. Spread the raspberry jam over the base and spread the coconut mixture evenly over the top
3. Place into the oven and bake for 15-20 minutes or until golden brown
4. Cool in tin and cut into squares

PORTABELLA MUSHROOM *fries*

 **PREP** 15 MINS **COOK** 30 MINS  **SERVES** 4-6

INGREDIENTS

FRIES

Vegetable oil, for deep-frying

100g (⅔ cup) plain flour

3 eggs, lighly beaten

2 cups panko breadcrumbs

250g Portabella Mushrooms, stalks trimmed, cut into thin fries

Salt and pepper, to season

HARISSA YOGHURT

2 tsp harissa

1 cup Greek-style yoghurt

METHOD

FRIES

1. Heat enough oil in a large saucepan to come one-third up the sides to 170°C.

2. Meanwhile, place the flour, eggs and breadcrumbs into 3 separate wide, shallow bowls.

3. Season the flour well with salt and pepper. Dust the mushroom fries in the flour, shaking off any excess, dip into the egg, then coat well in the breadcrumbs.

4. In batches, deep-fry the fries for 5 minutes or until golden and cooked. Drain well on paper towel and season with salt.

HARISSA YOGHURT

1. Mix harissa together with yoghurt. Serve with fries.

TIP AND HINTS:

You can also use large flat white mushrooms, if you prefer

WATERMELON CUBES WITH FETA, OLIVES
and mint

 **PREP** 20 MINS   **MAKES** 12

INGREDIENTS

½ small (about 2kg) piece seedless watermelon, chilled

100g Persian or marinated feta, drained

1 tbs finely chopped mint leaves, plus 12 small mint leaves, to serve

6 pitted Kalamata olives, finely chopped

Dukkah, to serve

METHOD

1. Trim watermelon and cut flesh into 12 x 3cm square cubes. Using a melon baller (or small knife), scoop a small well out of each watermelon cube, ensuring that you keep the watermelon sides intact.

2. Beat feta in a small bowl until smooth. Stir in mint and olives. Spoon mixture into watermelon cubes. Top each with a small mint leaf. Place onto a serving tray, sprinkle with dukkah and serve.

TIPS & HINTS:

Excellent for easy entertaining, serve these with cool drinks. Toss leftover watermelon through a fruit salad or blend it for an iced drink.
Dukkah is a delicious mixture of ground seeds, spices and nuts. It's available from some greengrocers and most supermarkets.

Tip

Cook meatballs
in batches for
even cooking

THAI PORK AND MUSHROOM
meatballs

 COOK 30 MINS **SERVES** 4

INGREDIENTS

400g button, cup or flat mushrooms

3 green onions, roughly chopped

3 tbs vegetable oil

2 tbs coriander paste or lightly
dried coriander

400g pork mince

2 tbs red curry paste

1 egg

1 cup fresh breadcrumbs

Vegetable oil, for cooking

Iceberg lettuce, sweet chilli sauce
and lime wedges, to serve

METHOD

1. Finely chop mushrooms by hand or alternatively,
   pulse in a food processor. Add chopped green onions
   to mushroom mixture.

2. Heat 1 tbs oil in a large non-stick frying pan over
   high heat. Add mushroom mixture and cook,
   stirring often, for 8 minutes or until all moisture has
   evaporated. Set aside to cool for 10 minutes. Drain
   any excess moisture and transfer mushrooms to a
   bowl. Wipe pan clean.

3. Add coriander paste to the mushrooms with the
   mince, curry paste, egg and breadcrumbs, mix until
   well combined.

4. Shape into balls with damp hands. Place onto a tray,
   cover and refrigerate 1 hour if time permits (this
   helps hold meatballs together when cooking).

5. Heat remaining oil in a large non-stick frying pan
   over medium heat. Cook meatballs, in batches for
   8-10 min, shaking pan often or until just cooked
   through. Serve with lettuce leaves, sweet chilli sauce
   and lime wedges.

CHEESE AND BACON PULL-APART *loaf*

 PREP 20 MINS  **COOK** 40 MINS **SERVES** 8

INGREDIENTS

150g (6 rashers) rindless streaky bacon, chopped

450g (3 cups) self-raising flour

90g cold Fairy Cooking Margarine, chopped into 1 cm pieces

125g (1¼ cups) grated mozzarella

150g (1¼ cups) grated vintage cheddar

2 eggs

180ml (¾ cups) milk

½ cup fresh parsley, chopped

METHOD

1. Preheat oven to 180°C (fan forced). Grease and line the base of a 20cm round tin with baking paper. Grease the sides of the tin.

2. Cook the bacon in a small frying pan over high heat for 2-3 minutes or until golden brown.

3. Put the flour in a large bowl. Add the Fairy Cooking Margarine and use your fingers to rub the margarine into the flour until sandy. Add 1 cup of mozzarella, 1 cup of cheddar and the bacon. Use a butter knife to mix until combined.

4. Beat the eggs and milk together. Add to the flour mixture and use a butter knife to stir together to form a dough. Turn out onto a floured kitchen bench and gently knead together. Divide into 8 balls.

5. Put the remaining mozzarella, remaining cheddar and parsley in a small bowl and mix to combine. Roll each of the balls of dough into the cheese mixture. Place into the prepared tin.

6. Bake for 35 minutes, or until the bread is golden brown and cooked.

TAPAS STYLE GARLIC *mushrooms*

 PREP 5 MINS **COOK** 10 MINS 👤 **SERVES** 2–4

INGREDIENTS

2 tbsp olive oil

250g button mushrooms, cleaned

4 garlic cloves, finely chopped

2 tsp smoked paprika

2 tbsp finely chopped parsley

Salt and pepper, to season

Aioli and lemon wedges, to serve

METHOD

1. Heat the oil in a large frying pan over medium-high heat. Cook the mushrooms for 5 minutes, tossing the pan regularly. Add the garlic, smoked paprika, salt and pepper and cook for a further 1-2 minutes or until golden, tossing the pan regularly. Toss through the parsley to combine

2. Serve the mushrooms with aioli and lemon wedges

" MAKE A MEAL OF IT AND SERVE MUSHROOMS WITH LOADS OF CRUSTY BREAD."

Top Tip

Scatter with chilli
flakes before
cooking for a kick!

BABY GREENS, CHERRY TOMATO AND PROSCIUTTO
pizza

 PREP 5 MINS **COOK** 15 MINS **MAKES** 1 LARGE

INGREDIENTS

1 large pizza base

3 tbsp tomato passata

5 slices prosciutto

½ cup mixed kale and spinach leaves

250g Perfect Italiano Perfect Pizza

½ cup cherry tomatoes, halved

8-10 basil leaves

Shaved Perfect Italiano Parmesan, to serve

METHOD

1. Preheat oven to 250°C.

2. Spread the pizza base with tomato passata. Arrange the prosciutto, cherry tomatoes, kale and spinach on top of pizza. Scatter with Perfect Italiano Perfect Pizza to evenly cover base.

3. Place the pizza in the oven for 10–15 minutes or until the cheese is melted and base is crispy. Remove from the oven, scatter with Perfect Italiano Shaved Parmesan and basil and serve immediately.

IF YOU PREFER, ADD THE PROSCIUTTO AFTER PIZZA HAS BEEN COOKED."

tip

Swap out the
salmon for ham
and the capers
for olives

SMOKED SALMON, RICOTTA AND ROCKET PITA
pizza

 **PREP** 5 MINS   **COOK** 15 MINS **MAKES** 1 LARGE

INGREDIENTS

1 medium pitta bread

2 tbsp tomato passata

100g Tassal Smoked Salmon

250g Perfect Italiano Perfect Pizza

1 tbsp Always Fresh Capers, drained

⅓ cup baby rocket leaves, to serve

⅓ cup Perfect Italiano Ricotta

Zest of half a lemon

METHOD

1. Preheat oven to 250°C.

2. Spread the pitta with tomato passata. Scatter with Perfect Italiano Perfect Pizza to evenly cover base.

3. Place the pizza in the oven for 10-15 minutes or until the cheese is melted and base is crispy. Remove from the oven, lay over slices of smoked salmon, sprinkle over capers, and rocket leaves. Dollop on spoonfuls of Perfect Italiano Ricotta, sprinkle over lemon zest and season with salt and pepper. Serve immediately.

Tip

Garnish with fresh
basil leaves and
a twist of lemon

EASY PRAWN
Pizza

 PREP 15 MINS   **COOK** 10 MINS   **SERVES** 4

INGREDIENTS

PIZZA

1 x any of the De Costi Prawn Range

½ pizza tomato paste

2 prepared thin pizza bases

1 cup pizza cheese

TO GARNISH

Fresh basil leaves

METHOD

PIZZA

1. Pre-heat oven 200°C.

2. Spread the tomato paste over the base and sprinkle the cheese evenly over the pizza base.

3. Mix De Costi Prawns in a bowl and divide evenly over the pizza bases.

4. Bake the pizzas for 5 minutes or until cheese is bubbly and beginning to look golden.

TO GARNISH

1. Slice pizza into wedges and garnish with basil leaves. Serve immediately.

TIPS & HINTS:

Spice up your pizza with a little chipotle mayonnaise for a delicious difference.

YELLOW NECTARINE, ARTICHOKE AND ROCKET
pizza

 **PREP** 25 MINS + PROVING TIME   **COOK** 15 MINS   **SERVES** 4

INGREDIENTS

¾ cup hot water

2 teaspoons instant yeast

1 teaspoon caster sugar

2 cups pizza flour

1 teaspoon sea salt flakes

⅓ cup olive oil

280g jar whole artichoke hearts, drained

½ cup finely grated parmesan

3 firm yellow nectarines, cut into thin wedges (approx. 180g each)

Shaved parmesan, to serve

20g baby rocket

⅓ cup balsamic glaze

METHOD

1. Whisk water, yeast and sugar in a jug and set aside for 10 minutes or until mixture is frothy. Place flour and salt into a large bowl. Add yeast mixture and 1 tablespoon oil. Stir until well combined and a soft dough forms. Turn onto a lightly floured surface and knead for 5 minutes or until a smooth dough forms. Place into an oiled bowl and set aside in a warm place for 30 minutes or until well risen.

2. Meanwhile, place artichoke, remaining ¼ cup oil, parmesan, salt and white pepper into a small food processor and pulse until a thick paste forms.

3. Preheat oven to 240°C. Grease 2 large baking trays. Punch down dough and divide in half. Roll one piece of dough on a lightly floured surface until approximately 25cm round. Place on prepared tray. Repeat with remaining dough.

4. Spread artichoke paste onto pizzas. Top with nectarine wedges and bake for 10-15 minutes or until pizza is golden and crisp. Top with shaved parmesan and rocket. Drizzle with balsamic glaze and serve immediately.

HAM, OLIVE, ASPARAGUS AND RICOTTA
pizza

 **PREP** 5MINS **COOK** 15 MINS **MAKES** 1 LARGE

INGREDIENTS

1 large pizza base

3 tbsp basil pesto

100g ham, torn into large pieces

½ bunch asparagus, trimmed and chopped into thirds

½ cup pitted kalamata olives

250g Perfect Italiano Perfect Pizza

⅓ cup Perfect Italiano Ricotta

6-8 basil leaves, to serve

METHOD

1. Preheat oven to 250°C.

2. Spread the pizza base with pesto. Arrange the ham, asparagus and olives on top of the pizza. Scatter with Perfect Italiano Perfect Pizza to evenly cover base.

3. Place the pizza in the oven for 10-15 minutes or until the cheese is melted and base is crispy. Remove from the oven and spoon over dollops of Perfect Italiano Ricotta and sprinkle over fresh basil leaves. Serve immediately.

CAULIFLOWER PIZZA WITH PESTO, SUMMER VEGGIES
and ricotta

PREP 5 MINS   **COOK** 15 MINS   **MAKES** 1 LARGE

INGREDIENTS

1 large cauliflower, florets removed and blitzed into rice (around 2 cups)

1 egg, lightly whisked

2 tbsp basil pesto and cashew dip

1 zucchini, trimmed and sliced into ribbons using a peeler

25g Perfect Italiano Grated Parmesan

250g Perfect Italiano Perfect Pizza

⅓ cup Perfect Italiano Ricotta

5-6 sorrel, to serve

METHOD

1. Preheat oven to 220°C.

2. To make the cauliflower crust, place cauliflower rice into a microwave safe bowl and microwave for 6-8 minutes or until very tender. Drain through a fine sieve and press down firmly with a spoon to remove all excess liquid (alternatively, wrap up in a clean chux and squeeze out all the excess liquid). Place cauliflower into a medium bowl and mix well with egg, parmesan and season with salt and pepper.

3. Line a baking tray with baking paper, and press cauliflower mixture firmly onto the tray forming a circle around 30cm. Place into the oven and bake for 20 minutes or until firm and golden. Remove from oven and allow to cool for 5 minutes.

4. Spread cauliflower base with basil pesto and cashew dip. Arrange the zucchini on top of pizza. Scatter with Perfect Italiano Perfect Pizza to evenly cover base.

5. Place the pizza in the oven for 10 minutes or until the cheese is melted and base is crispy. Remove from the oven, dollop spoonfuls of Perfect Italiano Ricotta on top of pizza, sprinkle over sorrel leaves and serve immediately.

BROCCOLINI & CAULIFLOWER FRIED 'RICE' & CHICKEN
bowls

 PREP 30 MINS   **COOK** 20 MINS   **SERVES** 4

INGREDIENTS

2 bunches broccolini, roughly chopped

600g cauliflower florets (about ½ large cauliflower)

¼ cup peanut oil

4 free-range eggs, at room temperature

4 long red chillies (leave whole)

400g chicken tenderloins, trimmed and cut into 2cm pieces

3 green onions (shallots), trimmed and thinly sliced, plus extra to serve

2 garlic cloves, finely chopped

150g green beans, cut into 3cm lengths

2 tbs kecap manis, plus extra to serve

1 cup trimmed bean sprouts

½ cup coriander leaves

chopped roasted peanuts, to serve

METHOD

1. Preheat oven to 100°C fan-forced. Using a food processor, pulse broccolini and cauliflower in batches until it resembles rice. Set aside.

2. Heat 1 tbs oil in a wok over high heat. Fry eggs one a time until crisp at the edges and whites are set. Transfer to a tray and keep warm in the oven. Add another 1 tbs oil to wok and fry chillies for 1-2 minutes until crisp. Transfer to the tray and keep warm in the oven.

3. Heat remaining 1 tbs oil in the wok over high heat. Add chicken and stir-fry for 2-3 minutes until white and sealed. Transfer to a plate. Add green onions, garlic and beans to wok and stir-fry for 1 minute. Toss through broccolini and cauliflower 'rice' and stir-fry for 2-3 minutes until just tender. Drizzle with kecap manis and toss to combine.

4. Spoon into serving bowls. Top each with an egg and a fried chilli. Sprinkle with bean sprouts, coriander and extra green onions. Serve with chopped roasted peanuts and extra kecap manis.

MANGO PRAWN *salad*

 PREP 15 MINS **SERVES** 2

INGREDIENTS

1 x 260g DeCosti Cooked Prawns
with Cocktail Sauce

1 fresh Ripe Mango, diced

½ Red Capsicum, finely diced

50g Rocket Leaves

GARNISH

Lime Wedge

METHOD

1. Add the diced Mango, DeCosti cooked prawns to a
   large bowl along with the diced capsicum and rocket
   leaves.

2. Open the dressing pack and squeeze in half the
   dressing. Gently toss the dressing through the prawn
   and mango mixture.

3. Serve the Mango Prawn salad garnish with a wedge
   of lime and a little extra dressing.

NOTES:

Salad maybe prepared ahead of time and dressed just
prior to serving.

LEMON AND GARLIC PRAWN
spaghetti

 PREP 7-10 MINS  **COOK** 6 MINS **MAKES** 4

INGREDIENTS

1 x 280g De Costi Prawns with Lemon & Garlic butter

½ packet of spaghetti, cooked and drained

1 tbsp of oil

Baby rocket, to serve

Fresh basil and sliced lemon, to serve

Salt and pepper, to season

METHOD

1. Heat the oil a small non-stick pan over a medium heat 2 minutes.

2. Add the De Costi Prawns to the pan and cook for 2 minutes then add the lemon & garlic butter for another 2 minutes.

3. Add the Prawns to the cooked pasta.

4. Toss through a handful of rocket. Garnish with fresh basil, sliced lemon and salt and pepper.

TIPS & HINTS:

Sprinkle with freshly grated parmesan for extra flavour.

 SPICE IT UP WITH FINELY CHOPPED RED CHILLI IF YOU LIKE IT HOT."

CARROT, TOMATO & CHICKEN QUINOA
salad

 PREP 20 MINS   **COOK** 30 MINS   **SERVES** 4-6

INGREDIENTS

1 cup white quinoa

1 small barbecued chicken

2 purple carrots

1 orange carrot

375g mixed baby tomatoes
(heirloom), quartered or halved

3 green onions (shallots), trimmed
and thinly sliced

½ cup small mint leaves, roughly
chopped

1 cup flat-leaf parsley leaves,
roughly chopped

½ cup shelled pistachio nuts,
roughly chopped

Lemon wedges, to serve

Lemon, tahini & yoghurt dressing

½ cup natural Greek-style yoghurt

1 tbs tahini

¼ cup lemon juice

METHOD

1. Place quinoa in a sieve and rinse in cold water.
   Combine quinoa and 2 cups water in medium
   saucepan and bring to the boil over medium-high
   heat. Reduce heat to low, cover and cook for
   15 minutes or until quinoa is cooked and water
   has been absorbed. Place quinoa into a large bowl.
   Set aside to cool slightly.

2. Meanwhile, shred chicken flesh, discarding skin and
   bones. Peel carrots. Using a julienne peeler or knife,
   shred carrots into long thin strips. Plunge carrots
   into a bowl of iced water. Stand for 5 minutes. Drain
   and pat dry carrots. Add chicken, carrots, tomatoes,
   green onions, mint, parsley and pistachios to quinoa.
   Toss to combine.

3. To make dressing, combine all ingredients in a bowl.
   Season with salt and pepper to taste. Whisk until
   well combined. Drizzle dressing over salad, gently
   toss and serve with lemon wedges.

Tip
....
This dish is delicious served hot or cold.

TOMATO AND GOAT'S CHEESE
tart

 PREP 1 HOUR   **COOK** 30 MINS **MAKES** 6 SLICES

INGREDIENTS

PASTRY

185g (1¼ cups) plain flour

¼ teaspoon baking powder

85g chilled Fairy margarine, cut into small pieces

1 egg yolk

1 tablespoon lemon juice

2–3 tablespoons cold water

FILLING

2 eggs

250 ml (1 cup) cream

Salt and pepper, to season

ASSEMBLY

250g cherry tomatoes, cut in half

150g goat's cheese

Basil leaves to garnish

METHOD

PASTRY

1. Combine flour, baking powder and Fairy in a food processor. Process until mixture resembles fine breadcrumbs. Add egg yolk, lemon juice and sufficient water until pastry comes together.

2. Knead lightly and pat into a round flat shape. Wrap in baking paper and place in the refrigerator for 30 minutes to rest.

3. Preheat oven to 200°C.

4. Roll dough out on a floured board and line a greased rectangular fluted fan tin.

5. Line with baking paper and fill with baking beans or rice. Rest in refrigerator for another 20 minutes.

6. Blind bake pastry for 10 minutes. Remove the paper and beans or rice, reduce the temperature to 180°C and bake for another 10 minutes or until golden.

FILLING

1. Lightly beat eggs and cream together, season with salt and pepper.

ASSEMBLY

1. Spread the cut tomatoes over the base and place chunks of goat's cheese over top.

2. Pour over the egg mix and bake for 10 minutes, reduce heat to 180°C and cook for a further 20 minutes or until filling is puffed and golden.

3. Top with fresh basil leaves to serve.

SOUTHERN-FRIED PORTABELLA MUSHROOM *burger*

 PREP 15 MINS  **COOK** 20 MINS **SERVES** 4

INGREDIENTS

Vegetable oil or other neutral oil, for shallow frying, plus extra for cooking

12 Portabella Mushrooms, stems removed

100g mozzarella, sliced (optional)

75g (½ cup) plain flour

2 tsp mixed dried herbs

3 eggs, lightly beaten

1 ½ cups fresh breadcrumbs

Salt and pepper, to season

Brioche burger buns, lettuce, tomato and horseradish mustard mayonnaise, to serve

METHOD

1. In batches, heat 1 tbsp of oil over medium-low heat. Cook the mushrooms for 5 minutes each or until cooked through. Transfer to a plate and allow to cool

2. Place 4 mushrooms with the underside facing up, add a slice of mozzarella, if using, to each, then top each with a mushroom. Add another slice of mozzerella then top with the remaining mushrooms with the tops facing up

3. Place the flour, eggs and breadcrumbs into 3 separate bowls. Stir the mixed herbs through the flour and season well with salt and pepper. Dust the mushroom patties well in the flour, then dip in the eggs to coat, then repeat process and coat well in the breadcrumbs

4. Add enough oil into a deep frying pan to come 2cm up the sides and heat to 180°C. Shallow fry the mushroom burgers for 3 minutes each side or until golden. Remove and drain well on paper towel, then season with salt and pepper

5. Serve the mushroom steaks with salad or in a burger

TIPS & HINTS:

You can also use large flat white mushrooms, if you prefer

PRAWN SOFT *tortillas*

 PREP 10 MINS   **COOK** 8 MINS **SERVES** 4

INGREDIENTS

PRAWN TORTILLAS

1 x any of the De Costi Flavoured Prawn range

6 mini soft tortillas, warmed

2 cups red cabbage slaw, thinly chopped

1 small Lebanese cucumber, thinly sliced

TO SERVE

Lime wedges

METHOD

PRAWN TORTILLAS

1. Heat a non-stick pan over medium heat for 2 minutes. Add the De Costi Flavoured Prawns to the pan and heat 1 minute.

2. Toss the prawns in the pan for 2–3 minutes until sizzling and prawns change colour and are opaque.

TO SERVE

1. Lay the warmed tortillas on a flat surface and place a small amount of red cabbage slaw onto each tortilla.

2. Top with a spoonful of cooked sweet chilli prawns, garnish with sliced cucumber and wedges of lime.

TIPS & HINTS:

This dish is delicious served warm or cold. Add avocado to the base of the tortillas and sour cream to serve.

HEALTHY PLUM
slice

 PREP 20 MINS **COOK** 55 MINS 👤 **MAKES** 12

INGREDIENTS

Filling

6 plums, stones removed, roughly chopped

2 tablespoons maple syrup

Base

2 cups rolled oats

1 cup almond meal

¼ cup maple syrup

2 tablespoons coconut oil

1 teaspoon sea salt flakes

1 teaspoon cinnamon

Topping

½ cup rolled oats

¼ cup slivered almonds

¼ cup pumpkin seeds

2 tablespoons sunflower seeds

1 tablespoon coconut oil

METHOD

Filling

1. Place plums and maple syrup into a saucepan and place over a medium heat. Bring mixture to the boil and simmer for 15-20 minutes until plums are soft, pulpy and firm. Cool. Place in fridge until required. (This can be made the day or night ahead of making.)

Base

1. Preheat oven to 180°C. Grease and line a 20cm x 20cm cake pan with baking paper.

2. To make the base place oats, almond meal, maple syrup, coconut oil, salt and cinnamon into a food processor and process until well combined and finely chopped. Press evenly over base of prepared cake pan. Bake for 15 minutes. Cool.

Topping

1. Spread plum mixture over cold base. For topping, combine oats, almonds, pumpkin seeds, sunflower seeds and coconut oil in a bowl. Stir until combined.

2. Sprinkle mixture over plums, pressing lightly. Bake for 20 minutes or until topping is light golden. Cool in pan. Remove from pan and cut into bars or squares.

3. Store in an airtight container in the refrigerator for up to 5 days.

PLAY **VIDEO**

CHERRY COCONUT CHEESECAKE WITH
chocolate crackle base

 PREP 30 MINS, PLUS 1 HOUR, 15 MINS SETTING TIME **SERVES** 12

INGREDIENTS

CHOCOLATE CRACKLE BASE

60g (¼ cup) Copha, chopped

60g dark chocolate, chopped

80g (½ cup) icing sugar mixture, sifted

2 tablespoons cocoa powder

50g (1 ⅔ cup) Kellogg's Rice Bubbles

20g (⅓ cup) desiccated coconut

CHEESECAKE FILLING

300g (1 ½ cups) cherries, pitted and halved

60ml (¼ cup) water

160g (1 cup) icing sugar mixture, sifted

500g cream cheese, chopped and softened

270ml can coconut cream

3 teaspoons powdered gelatine

CHOC-CHERRY TOPPING

100g dark chocolate, chopped

20g (1 tablespoon) Copha

12 cherries, extra

METHOD

CHOCOLATE CRACKLE BASE

1. Grease and line the base and sides of a 22cm spring form cake tin. In a heatproof bowl, combine chocolate and Copha. Place over a pot of lightly simmering water. Stir until melted. Remove from heat.

2. Place sugar, cocoa, rice bubbles and coconut in a large bowl. Add Copha mixture and mix to combine. Press into base of tin. Put in fridge to set for 10 minutes.

CHEESECAKE FILLING

3. Place cherries, sugar, water in a small saucepan over high heat. Bring to the boil and cook for 4 minutes, to soften. Remove from the heat and cool slightly for 5 minutes. Using a stick blender, blend until smooth.

4. Sprinkle over the gelatine and set aside for 5 minutes to dissolve. Mix until smooth. Set aside.

5. Place cheese in large bowl and using hand-held beaters, beat for 4 minutes until light and fluffy. Add coconut cream and beat for 4 minutes until light and smooth. Strain the cherry mixture through a sieve and gradually add to the cheese mixture. Stir to combine. Pour over base and put in fridge to set for 1 hour.

CHOC-CHERRY TOPPING

6. In a heatproof bowl, combine the chocolate and Copha. Place over a pot of lightly simmering water. Stir occasionally until melted. Remove from heat.

7. Half dip the cherries in the chocolate, place on baking paper and refrigerate for 2 minutes to set.

1. Remove cheesecake from tin and drizzle with chocolate mixture. Top with cherries to serve.

Tip

This easy no bake slice is a summer favourite

LEMON COCONUT
slice

 **PREP** 30 MINS   **MAKES** 24 BARS

INGREDIENTS

BASE

125g (½ block) Copha, chopped

250g (1 packet) Arnott's Milk Coffee Biscuits

80g (1 cup) desiccated coconut

160g (½ cup) sweetened condensed milk

LEMON TOPPING

185g (¾ cup) Copha, chopped

110g (¾ cup) white chocolate melts

200g (⅔ cup) sweetened condensed milk

250g tub sour cream

60ml (¼ cup) lemon juice

2 teaspoons finely grated lemon rind

40g (½ cup) desiccated coconut, extra

1 teaspoon finely grated lemon rind, extra

METHOD

BASE

1. Grease and line a 20cm x 30cm slice tin. Make sure the paper has a 2cm overhang

2. Melt the Copha in a microwave on high or in a saucepan until fully melted. Using a food processor process the biscuits and coconut until they resemble fine breadcrumbs

3. Add the melted Copha and sweetened condensed milk and mix together. Press the biscuit mixture firmly into the tin, using the back of a spoon. Put in the fridge to set for 10 minutes

LEMON TOPPING

1. Melt the Copha and chocolate in a microwave on high or in a saucepan over low heat until fully melted and combined

2. Place sweetened condensed milk, sour cream, lemon juice and rind in a large bowl and mix to combine. Add the Copha chocolate mixture and mix until smooth

3. Pour over the base and smooth the top. Put in the fridge to set for 20 minutes

4. Place extra coconut and lemon rind in a small bowl and mix to combine. Sprinkle over the slice to serve. Slice into 24 bars

TIPS & HINTS

This slice will keep in an airtight container in the fridge for up to 3 days

PEACH, COCONUT AND HAZELNUT *loaf*

PREP 15 MINS   **COOK** 10 MINS   **MAKES** 1 LOAF

INGREDIENTS

125g butter, softened

⅔ cup caster sugar

1 teaspoon vanilla extract

2 eggs, at room temperature

1 cup sour cream

2 yellow peaches, stone removed, finely diced

1½ cups self-raising flour

½ cup plain flour

½ cup desiccated coconut

⅓ cup roasted hazelnuts, finely chopped

METHOD

1. Preheat oven to 180°C. Grease a 6 cup-capacity (20cm x 10cm x 7cm deep base measurement) loaf pan and line with baking paper, 5cm above line of pan. Using an electric mixer, beat butter, sugar and vanilla until pale and creamy. Add egg, 1 at a time, beating well after each addition.

2. Using a large metal spoon, gently fold in sour cream, peaches and coconut. Sift flours over batter and gently fold until combined.

3. Spoon batter into prepared loaf pan. Smooth top and sprinkle with chopped nuts, pressing gently into batter. Bake for 1 hour or until a skewer inserted into the centre comes out clean. Stand for 10 minutes before turning out onto a wire rack to cool.

NECTARINE AND APRICOT COCONUT
chia puddings

PREP 25　**SERVES** 4

INGREDIENTS

2 x 270m cans coconut milk

¾ cup white chia seeds

1 teaspoon vanilla extract

4 yellow nectarines, stone removed, cut into thin wedges

4 apricots, stone removed, finely diced

½ cup maple syrup, to serve

¼ cup toasted flaked coconut, to serve

METHOD

1. Place coconut milk, chia seeds and vanilla into a bowl and stir until well combined. Set aside for 15 minutes to thicken.

2. Spoon half the chia mixture into the base of 4 x 1 cup-capacity glasses or glass bowls. Top with half the nectarines and apricots. Spoon remaining chia seed mixture over fruit. Place remaining fruit onto chia seed mixture.

3. Place in refrigerator for 1 hour or until cold. Drizzle the maple syrup over the fruit. Sprinkle with coconut and serve.

NO-BAKE BLUEBERRY & SWEET RICOTTA *tart*

 PREP 25 MINS + CHILLING TIME 👤 **SERVES** 8

INGREDIENTS

Biscuit base

250g Butternut Snap or Marie biscuits

125g unsalted butter, melted

Ricotta cannoli filling

500g fresh ricotta

⅓ cup icing sugar, plus extra for dusting

½ tsp vanilla extract

250g blueberries

Finely shredded orange zest and honey, to serve

METHOD

1. To make the biscuit base, place biscuits into a food processor and process until finely chopped. Add butter and process until well combined.

2. Evenly press mixture into the base of 22cm wide x 2.5cm deep loose-base fluted tart pan. Refrigerate for 3 hours (or longer if time permits).

3. To make the filling, place ricotta, icing sugar and vanilla into a medium bowl. Using electric hand beaters, beat the mixture until smooth. Cover and chill until ready to serve.

4. Just before serving, fill the tart case with the ricotta mixture. Scatter with blueberries. Dust with icing sugar and sprinkle with orange zest. Drizzle with a little honey and serve.

top tip

Easy and mild butter chicken idea for kids.

MILD BUTTER CHICKEN
roti bowls

 PREP 5 MINS **COOK** 25 MINS  **SERVES** 4

INGREDIENTS

6 mini roti, warmed following
packet directions

1 tablespoon vegetable oil

6 chicken thigh fillets, diced

1 brown onion, diced

375g Passage to India Extra Mild
Butter Chicken Simmer Sauce

200g frozen peas

Yoghurt, to serve

Coriander leaves, optional, to serve

METHOD

1. Preheat oven to 180°C / 160°C fan-forced. Spray roti with olive oil cooking spray and press into a 6-hole Texan muffin pan. Bake in the oven for 12-14 minutes or until golden brown.

2. Meanwhile, heat oil in a large non-stick frying pan over medium heat. Add chicken and cook for 5-6 minutes or until browned on all sides. Transfer to a plate. Drain excess fat and discard.

3. Add onion and cook for 5 minutes or until softened. Pour Passage to India Extra Mild Butter Chicken Simmer Sauce and ¼ cup water into pan and bring to a simmer. Return chicken to pan, coating well with sauce. Cover, reduce heat and simmer for 10 minutes or until chicken is cooked through, adding peas for the last 2 minutes.

4. Spoon butter chicken into roti bowls. Serve with yoghurt and coriander, if you like.

TIPS & HINTS:

You can also serve with steamed basmati rice to make it a heartier meal.

BAKED
mac & cheese

 PREP 10 MINS   **COOK** 35 MINS **SERVES** 4

INGREDIENTS

500 g macaroni

60 g (3 tbsps.) Western Star Original Butter

¼ cup plain flour

3 cups (750 ml) milk, warmed

2½ cups (135 g) Perfect Bakes cheese

2 tbsps. oregano leaves, chopped

1½ cups panko breadcrumbs

¼ cup (60 ml) olive oil

METHOD

1. Preheat oven to 200°C / 180°C fan-forced. Grease a 2 litre (8 cup capacity) ovenproof dish.

2. Cook pasta in a large saucepan according to packet instructions for 12 minutes or until tender. Refresh under cold water. Drain well.

3. Meanwhile, melt butter in a saucepan over medium heat. Slowly add the flour, whisking until combined. Add the milk in batches and continue to stir until the sauce becomes thick and coats the back of a wooden spoon. Stir in 1½ cups of Perfect Bakes cheese.

4. Add cooked pasta and oregano to the sauce, stir to combine. Spoon into the prepared dish.

5. Place panko and remaining 1 cup of Perfect Bakes cheese in a medium bowl. Pour in the oil and use your hands to mix until well combined. Scatter crumb mix over the pasta and bake for 20 minutes or until golden brown. Serve with a simple salad of your choice.

101

Tip

This recipe is so quick and easy as you can use any leftover Bolognese sauce to make it.

BOLOGNESE
pasta bake

 PREP 5 MINS **COOK** 35 MINS 👤 **SERVES** 4-6

INGREDIENTS

500 g rigatoni pasta

20 g (1 tbsp) Western Star Original Butter

3 cups any leftover Bolognese sauce, warmed

2½ cups (225 g) Perfect Bakes cheese

METHOD

1. Preheat oven to 200°C / 180°C fan-forced. Grease a 3 litre (12 cup capacity) ovenproof dish.

2. Cook the pasta in a large saucepan according to packet instructions for 12 minutes or until tender. Drain well.

3. Add the pasta to prepared dish along with the butter and toss to combine. Add the bolognese and half the Perfect Bakes cheese, stirring through gently to combine. Top with remaining Perfect Bakes cheese. Bake for 20 minutes or until the cheese is melted and golden brown. Allow to rest for a few minutes before serving.

RECIPE NOTE:

Prep and cook times based on using leftover Bolognese.

EASY AVOCADO
parmigiana

 PREP 10 MINS **COOK** 15 MINS 👤 **SERVES** 4

INGREDIENTS

4 chicken breast fillets

⅓ cup plain flour

2 eggs, lightly whisked

1 cup Panko breadcrumbs

2 tablespoons Dijon mustard

1 just-ripe avocado, skin and seed removed, sliced

4 slices Swiss cheese

METHOD

1. Preheat oven to 200°C / 180°C fan-forced. Grease and line a baking tray with baking paper.

2. Place 1 chicken breast between 2 sheets of baking paper. Gently flatten with a rolling pin to ½ cm thick. Repeat with remaining chicken.

3. Coat each chicken breast in flour, shake off excess. Then dip in egg, and press into breadcrumbs, coating both sides.

4. Heat an oiled non-stick frying pan with enough oil to shallow fry. Add chicken and cook for about 2 minutes on each side or until golden.

5. Transfer to prepared tray. Evenly spread mustard over the top side of the chicken. Top with sliced avocado and then the cheese.

6. Bake for 7-8 minutes or until cooked through.

7. Remove from oven and serve with a simple salad.

SRI LANKAN COCONUT & CASHEW
with saffron rice

 PREP 5 MINS   **COOK** 25 MINS   **SERVES** 4

INGREDIENTS

2 tablespoons vegetable oil

750g chicken thigh fillet, cut into 3cm cubes

375g Passage to India Sri Lankan Coconut & Cashew Chicken Simmer Sauce

150g green beans, trimmed and halved

165ml can coconut milk

½ teaspoon saffron threads

1 brown onion, finely diced

2 garlic cloves, finely chopped

1 cup basmati rice, rinsed

1 bunch coriander, sprigs removed

⅓ cup cashews, roughly chopped

¼ cup toasted flaked coconut

METHOD

1. Heat 1 tablespoon oil in a large non-stick frying pan over medium high heat. Add chicken and cook for 8 minutes or until browned. Add Passage to India Sri Lankan Coconut & Cashew Chicken Simmer Sauce and bring to the boil. Reduce heat and simmer for 15 minutes, adding beans for final 5 minutes, or until chicken is cooked through. Stir through coconut milk.

2. Meanwhile, place saffron into a small bowl and cover with 2 tablespoons boiling water. Stand for 5 minutes.

3. Heat remaining oil in a saucepan over medium heat. Add onion and garlic and cook for 4 minutes or until softened. Add rice, saffron and 2 cups water. Bring mixture to the boil, reduce heat and simmer for 8 minutes. Remove from heat and cover. Stand for 5 minutes. Roughly chop half the coriander and stir through rice. Season.

4. Spoon saffron rice onto serving plates. Top with curry, cashews and toasted coconut.

Tip

Don't have spreadable? Use butter instead.

MUSHROOM RAGU WITH
creamy polenta

 PREP 20 MINS   **COOK** 15 MINS   **SERVES** 4

INGREDIENTS

MUSHROOM RAGU

80 g (about ⅓ cup) Western Star Spreadable Original Soft

1 leek, washed and sliced

2 garlic cloves, crushed

200 g field mushrooms, sliced

200 g Swiss brown mushrooms, sliced

200 g cup button mushrooms, sliced

6 sprigs of thyme

185 ml (¾ cup) vegetable stock

2 teaspoons cornflour

50 g baby spinach leaves

Roughly chopped flat-leaf parsley, to serve

POLENTA

500 ml (2 cups) milk

500 ml (2 cups) vegetable stock

⅔ cup instant polenta

20 g (1 tablespoon) Western Star Spreadable Original Soft

½ cup shredded parmesan, plus extra for serving

METHOD

MUSHROOM RAGU

1. Melt the Spreadable in a large frying pan over medium-high heat. Add the leek and garlic and sauté for 2-3 minutes or until the leeks are softened. Add mushrooms and thyme. Cook for 5 minutes, stirring gently so as to not break up mushrooms.

2. Combine stock with the cornflour and stir into mushroom mixture. Cook over medium heat for a further 3-4 minutes or until the sauce has thickened slightly. Fold through the spinach and remove from heat. Season to taste with salt and pepper.

POLENTA

1. Combine milk and stock in a medium heavy-based saucepan over high heat and bring to the boil. Reduce heat to medium and gradually add polenta, stirring constantly. Cook, stirring constantly, for about 3 minutes or until polenta is soft and smooth. Remove from heat. Stir in Spreadable and parmesan.

2. To serve, spoon the creamy polenta onto serving plates and top with the mushroom ragu. Scatter with a little extra parmesan and the parsley.

NOTE:

If your polenta is thick rather than creamy, use a little extra hot milk to thin it down until you get to your desired consistency.

CHICKEN MEATBALLS IN A CREAMY
mushroom sauce

PREP 10 MINS **COOK** 20 MINS **SERVES** 4

INGREDIENTS

1 x 500 g packet dried fettuccine

500 g chicken mince

1½ cups soft fresh breadcrumbs (see Note)

1 egg, lightly whisked

250 g tub   Ricotta

1 garlic clove, crushed

1 cup (100 g) Perfect Italiano™ Parmesan Grated

2 tbsps. olive oil

150 g cup button mushrooms, thickly sliced

150 g brown mushrooms, quartered

300 ml thickened cream

2 tbsps. Worcestershire sauce

Finely chopped flat-leaf parsley, to serve

METHOD

1. Cook the fettuccine according to packet instructions. Drain and then set aside.

2. Combine the chicken mince, breadcrumbs, egg, Ricotta, garlic and ⅔ cup of the parmesan in a large bowl. Season. Shape into 16 meatballs.

3. Heat half the oil in a large non-stick fry pan over medium-high heat. In 2 batches, cook meatballs, turning occasionally, for 5 minutes or until browned all over. Transfer to a plate.

4. Heat remaining oil in pan. Add mushrooms and cook, stirring occasionally, for 8 minutes or until tender. Add cream, remaining parmesan and Worcestershire sauce and bring to the boil. Reduce heat to medium. Add the meatballs and cook for 5 minutes or until meatballs are cooked through and the sauce thickens slightly.

5. Add cooked pasta to the sauce and serve sprinkled with parsley.

RECIPE NOTES:

To freeze meatballs, cook completely at end of step 2. Cool and place in resealable plastic food storage bags. Label, date and freeze for up to 3 months. Thaw in fridge overnight. Reduce cooking time in step 3 to 3 minutes.

Fresh breadcrumbs help to keep the meatballs moist and from falling apart during cooking. Simply process 3 slices of day-old bread for the breadcrumbs.

SPICY CHESTNUT, PUMPKIN & *pancetta soup*

 PREP 20 MINS **COOK** 40 MINS **SERVES** 4

INGREDIENTS

CHESTNUTS

700g fresh chestnuts (to make 500g chestnuts for soup recipe below)

SOUP

1½ tbsp olive oil

100g sliced pancetta, chopped

1 brown onion, finely chopped

2 celery stalks, sliced

2 garlic cloves, chopped

2 long red chillies, deseeded and chopped

500g cooked and peeled chestnuts (prepped from fresh in part one of recipe)

750g peeled and chopped butternut pumpkin

5 cups chicken stock

Reduced fat sour cream and extra sliced long red chilli, to serve

METHOD

CHESTNUTS

1. Preheat oven to 200°C / 180°C fan-forced.

2. Cut a shallow cross into the flat side of each chestnut shell. Place prepared chestnuts onto a baking tray and bake for 15-20 minutes or until the shells split open.

3. Once cooked, remove chestnuts from heat and wrap in a clean tea towel for 5 minutes. While chestnuts are still warm, quickly peel off the outer brown shell and remove the papery thin skin underneath.

SOUP

4. Heat 2 tsp oil in a large saucepan over medium-high heat. Add the pancetta and cook, stirring often, for 3 minutes, until crispy. Transfer to a plate. Set aside.

5. Heat the remaining 1 tbsp oil in the pan over medium heat. Add onion, celery, garlic and chillies and cook, stirring often, for 4-5 minutes until softened.

6. Add chestnuts and pumpkin, and cook, stirring occasionally, for 5 minutes. Stir in the stock and three-quarters of the pancetta. Cover and bring to the boil. Reduce heat, cover and simmer, stirring occasionally, for 20-25 minutes until pumpkin and chestnuts are tender.

7. Puree soup with a stick blender until smooth. Season to taste. Cover and bring to the boil over medium heat. Ladle soup into serving bowls. Top each with a dollop of sour cream, the remaining pancetta and extra sliced red chilli and serve.

Top Tip
Ask your butcher to cut up the chicken for you.

CHICKEN, AVOCADO & CRUNCHY
potato tray bake

 PREP 10 MINS   **COOK** 45 MINS **SERVES** 4

INGREDIENTS

1 x 1.8kg chicken, cut into 8 pieces

2 tablespoons olive oil, plus
extra to drizzle

3 garlic cloves, crushed

salt and pepper

1 lemon, juiced

6 sprigs oregano

750g baby chat potatoes, halved

1 lemon, sliced

250g green beans, blanched
and halved

2 avocados, cut into wedges

2 cups baby spinach leaves

100g fetta, crumbled

METHOD

1. Preheat oven to 220°C / 200°C fan-forced.

2. Put the chicken, oil, garlic, salt, pepper, lemon juice
   and oregano in a large bowl and mix to combine.
   Set aside to marinate.

3. Place the potatoes on a large oven tray and cook in
   oven for 15 minutes or until golden brown. Top with
   the marinated chicken, marinade and lemon slices.
   Cook for 28-30 minutes or until golden brown and
   cooked through.

4. To serve, top with beans, avocado and spinach.
   Crumble with fetta and drizzle with oil.

tip

If the lamb is browning too quickly, cover with foil.

KORMA MARINATED LAMB SHOULDER
with spinach lentils

 PREP 5 MINS   **COOK** 4 HRS 👤 **SERVES** 4

INGREDIENTS

1.6kg shoulder of lamb, with bone

375g Passage to India Korma Simmer Sauce

2 tablespoons vegetable oil

1 brown onion, diced

1 cup brown lentils, rinsed

2 cups chicken stock

120g bag baby spinach leaves

1 bunch coriander, sprigs removed

steamed basmati rice, to serve

1 cup thick Greek-style yoghurt

METHOD

1. Using a sharp knife, make 4 diagonal slashes on both sides of lamb. Place into a roasting pan. Pour the Passage to India Korma Simmer Sauce over one side of lamb and, using your fingers, rub into slashes and all over meat. Cover and refrigerate overnight to marinate.

2. Preheat oven to 160°C / 140°C fan-forced. Remove roasting pan from refrigerator and stand for 20 minutes for meat to come to room temperature. Drizzle half the oil over lamb and pour in ½ cup water. Roast for 3 hours (cover with foil if lamb is browning too much). Add onion, lentils and stock to lamb, cover with foil and roast for a further 1 hour or until lentils are cooked and lamb is pull-apart tender.

3. Transfer lamb to a serving platter and cover loosely to rest. Stir spinach into lentils until just wilted. Spoon lentil mixture around lamb. Sprinkle with coriander sprigs and serve with rice and yoghurt.

TIKKA MASALA
vegetarian pies

 PREP 10 MINS   **COOK** 45 MINS 👤 **SERVES** 4

INGREDIENTS

1 tablespoon vegetable oil

1 brown onion, finely diced

1 carrot, finely diced

375g Passage to India Tikka Masala Simmer Sauce

1 zucchini, finely diced

1½ cups broccoli florets

100g green beans, cut into 2cm pieces

1 cob of corn, kernels removed

4 sheets ready rolled frozen puff pastry

1 egg, whisked

1 tablespoon sesame seeds

mango chutney, to serve

METHOD

1. Heat oil in a large non-stick frying pan over medium heat. Add onion and carrot and cook for 5 minutes or until softened. Add Passage to India Tikka Masala Simmer Sauce and ⅓ cup water. Bring to the boil.

2. Add zucchini, broccoli, green beans and corn. Stir until well combined. Cook for 4 minutes or until tender. Cool.

3. Preheat oven to 200°C / 180°C fan-forced. Place a baking tray in oven. Grease 4 metal pie tins. Cut 4 x 13cm rounds from pastry. Line prepared tins with pastry. Spoon vegetable curry mixture into pie shells. Cut 4 x 12cm rounds from pastry. Brush edge of pastry shell with water. Cover pie filling with pastry rounds and seal. Brush top of pies with egg and sprinkle with sesame seeds. Cut a small cross on the top of each pie. Place pies onto hot tray and bake for 25 minutes or until golden and crisp.

4. Serve pies with mango chutney.

Tip

Kecap manis is a sweet soy sauce available in the Asian section of supermarkets or from Asian grocers.

ROASTED ASIAN STYLE CHICKEN
with chestnuts

 PREP 20 MINS   **COOK** 1 HOUR **SERVES** 4

INGREDIENTS

ROASTED CHESTNUTS
570g uncooked chestnuts to make 400g cooked chestnuts

ASIAN-STYLE CHICKEN
¼ cup kecap manis

⅓ cup sweet chilli sauce

1 tsp sesame oil

2 garlic cloves, finely chopped

2 tsp finely grated fresh ginger

2 tbs lime juice

8 chicken thighs (bone in), fat trimmed

400g roasted chestnuts

¼ cup coriander leaves

Steamed rice and Asian greens, to serve

METHOD

ROASTED CHESTNUTS
1. Preheat oven to 200°C / 180°C fan-forced. Cut a shallow cross into flat side of each chestnut shell.

2. Place prepared chestnuts onto a baking tray. Bake for 15-20 minutes or until the shells split open.

3. Once cooked, remove chestnuts from the heat and wrap in a clean tea towel for 5-10 minutes. While chestnuts are still warm, quickly peel outer brown shell and remove the papery thin skin underneath.

ASIAN-STYLE CHICKEN
1. Combine kecap manis, sweet chilli sauce, sesame oil, garlic, ginger and lime juice in a bowl.

2. Place kecap manis mixture, chicken and chestnuts into a large snap-lock plastic bag. Toss to coat chicken and chestnuts in mixture. Seal and refrigerate for 1 hour (or longer if time permits).

3. Preheat oven to 220°C / 200°C fan-forced. Transfer chicken and chestnut mixture to a large baking pan lined with non-stick baking paper. Roast, turning occasionally, for 30-35 minutes or until chicken is golden and cooked through in the thickest part.

4. Remove from oven, sprinkle with coriander. Serve with steamed rice and Asian greens.

MEXICAN
lasagne

 PREP 15 MINS **COOK** 45 MINS  **SERVES** 6

INGREDIENTS

1 x 375 g jar mild tomato salsa

1 tbsp. olive oil

1 brown onion, finely chopped

750 g beef mince

35 g sachet taco seasoning

1 x 400 g can diced tomatoes

1 x 250 g packet microwave white rice, heated

1 red capsicum, chopped

1 x 420 g can corn kernels, rinsed

1 x 400 g can black beans, rinsed

2 spring onions, sliced

9 regular flour tortillas

3 cups (270 g)
4 Cheese Melt

METHOD

1. Preheat oven to 200°C / 180°C fan-forced. Grease a 30cm x 20cm (10 cup capacity) rectangular ovenproof dish. Spread half of the salsa over base of prepared dish.

2. Heat half of the oil in a large non-stick fry pan over medium heat. Add onion and cook, stirring for 3 minutes or until soft. Add mince and cook, stirring to break up lumps, for 5 minutes or until browned. Add taco seasoning and cook, stirring for 30 seconds or until fragrant. Add canned tomatoes and bring to the boil then reduce heat and simmer for 5 minutes. Stir in rice and remove from heat.

3. Heat remaining oil in a second non-stick fry pan over medium heat. Add capsicum and cook, stirring for 3 minutes or until tender. Stir in corn, beans and spring onion. Remove from heat.

4. Place 3 tortillas over base of prepared dish to cover. Top with half of the mince mixture, then a third of the corn mixture and a third of the 4 Cheese Melt. Top with another 3 tortillas, then remaining mince mixture, half of the remaining corn mixture and half of the remaining 4 Cheese Melt. Top with remaining tortillas.

5. Spread tortillas with remaining tomato salsa. Top with remaining corn mixture. Then sprinkle with remaining 4 Cheese Melt. Bake for 35 minutes or until golden brown. Stand for 5 minutes before cutting.

Tip

Add sliced button mushrooms to the dish with the potatoes.

CREAMY ONE POT
roast chicken

 PREP 30 MINS   **COOK** 90 MINS   **SERVES** 4

INGREDIENTS

1 large leek, pale section only, cut into 2 cm pieces

1 x approx. 1.6 kg fresh butterflied chicken

60 g (3 tablespoons) Western Star Spreadable Original Soft

1 tablespoon chopped thyme, plus extra sprigs, to serve

1 lemon, rind finely grated

2 garlic cloves, crushed

300 ml Western Star Thickened Cream

185 ml (¾ cup) chicken stock

1 tablespoon mustard powder

3 teaspoons brown sugar

500 g baby chat potatoes, quartered

Roughly chopped flat-leaf parsley, to serve

METHOD

1. Preheat oven to 200°C / 180°C fan-forced. Scatter the leek over the base of a large round flame-proof baking dish. Top with the chicken, breast side up.

2. Combine the Spreadable, thyme, lemon rind and garlic in a small bowl. Spread over the chicken and season with salt and pepper. Roast for 30 minutes.

3. Whisk together the cream, stock, mustard and brown sugar in a jug until well combined. Add the potatoes to the chicken at the 30 minute mark and pour the cream mixture over the chicken and potatoes. Roast for a further 45 minutes or until the chicken is golden and cooked through.

4. Carve and serve the chicken with the potatoes and the creamy sauce drizzled over. Scatter with fresh parsley and extra thyme sprigs to serve.

NOTES:

If you have a larger or smaller chicken, adjust cooking time accordingly until chicken is cooked through. You can check by piercing the chicken thigh near the bone, if the juices run clear, the chicken is cooked.

If you prefer a thicker sauce, transfer chicken and potatoes to a plate and cover loosely with foil to keep warm. Combine 2 teaspoons cornflour and 2 tablespoons of water in a jug and add to the creamy pan juices. Stir over medium heat until sauce thickens.

CHOC-ORANGE 'BREAD & BUTTER' *pudding*

 PREP 15 MINS   **COOK** 50-60 MINS   **SERVES** 6-8

INGREDIENTS

8 slices brioche loaf

80 g (about ⅓ cup) Western Star Spreadable Original Soft

½ cup orange or blood orange marmalade

600 ml Western Star Thickened Cream, plus extra, to serve

4 eggs

½ cup brown sugar

2 teaspoons vanilla

100g dark or milk chocolate, chopped into chunks

METHOD

1. Preheat oven to 160°C / 145°C fan-forced.

2. Spread both sides of the brioche slices with the Spreadable, then spread only one side of each slice with the marmalade. Cut each slice in half and place overlapping, marmalade side up, into the base of a round 8-cup capacity baking dish.

3. In a bowl, whisk together the cream, eggs, brown sugar and vanilla then pour over the bread. Dot the chocolate chunks among the brioche slices, then stand for 10 minutes.

4. Bake for 50-60 minutes or until the custard has just set. Serve warm with extra cream.

RAW AVOCADO
slice

 PREP 15 MINS + FREEZER TIME   **MAKES** 24

INGREDIENTS

BASE

1 cup raw cashews

1 cup oats (LOWAN)

1 packet fresh pitted medjool dates

2 tbs cacao powder

¼ coconut oil, melted

AVOCADO FILLING

4 cups shredded coconut

1 tbs coconut sugar

¼ cup Natvia

2 Avocados

¾ cup coconut oil, melted and cooled

CHOC TOP

2 tablespoons cacao powder

⅔ cup coconut oil, melted and cooled

⅓ cup maple syrup

METHOD

BASE

1. Put cashews and oats in a food processor and blitz to make a rough crumb (not too chunky). Add the dates, cacao and a pinch of salt. Blend the mixture and slowly add the coconut oil to bring the mix together. You may not need all the coconut oil. Press mix evenly into a slice pan, lined with baking paper and transfer to the freezer to firm up.

AVOCADO FILLING

1. Place all ingredients in a clean food processor bowl and blitz to combine to desired consistency. Add to prepared base. Return to freezer to set for at least 30 minutes before adding the chocolate top.

CHOC TOP

1. Combine all ingredients in a bowl and pour over the top of avocado slice. Return slice to freezer for 1-2 hours until slice is completely set.

GLUTEN-FREE CHESTNUT
& chocolate brownies

 PREP 20 MINS **COOK** 25-30 MINS  **MAKES** 16

INGREDIENTS

CHESTNUTS
500g fresh chestnuts

BROWNIES
350g cooked and peeled chestnuts

Standard self-raising flour can be used for a non-gluten free version.

200g good quality dark chocolate, broken into squares

200g unsalted butter, chopped

1 ¼ cups brown sugar

1 tsp vanilla extract

4 eggs, lightly beaten

½ cup gluten-free self-raising flour

2 tbsp cocoa

Pinch salt

METHOD

CHESTNUTS
1. Preheat oven to 200°C / 180°C fan-forced.

2. Cut a shallow cross into the flat side of each chestnut shell. Place prepared chestnuts onto a baking tray and bake for 15 to 20 minutes or until the shells split open.

3. Remove chestnuts from the heat and wrap in a clean tea towel for 5 minutes. While chestnuts are still warm, quickly peel off the outer brown shell and remove the papery thin skin underneath.

BROWNIES
1. Reduce oven to 180°C / 160°C fan-forced. Grease and line a 16cm x 26cm x 2-3cm deep slab pan with baking paper, leaving a 2cm overhang on the sides.

2. Set aside 50g cooked and peeled chestnuts. Place remaining chestnuts into a food processor. Process until fine crumbs form (you'll need 2 cups ground chestnuts). Set aside.

3. Place chocolate and butter in a large microwave safe bowl and microwave on high for 2 minutes, stirring with a metal spoon every minute until melted. Set aside to cool.

4. Using a metal spoon, stir in sugar, vanilla and eggs into chocolate mixture until well combined. Sift over flour, cocoa and salt. Stir to combine. Gently fold through chestnuts. Pour into prepared pan. Chop reserved chestnuts and sprinkle over mixture. Bake for 25-30 minutes until a skewer inserted comes out with moist crumbs sticking. Cool completely in the pan. Cut into squares. Serve with whipped cream and a dusting of cocoa if liked.

APPLE & MIXED BERRY CRUMBLE
with orange custard

 PREP 20 MINS 🍲 **COOK** 45 MINS 👤 **SERVES** 6

INGREDIENTS

APPLE-BERRY MIXTURE

60 g Western Star Chef's Choice Unsalted Cultured Butter

¼ cup caster sugar

4 granny smith apples, peeled, quartered and sliced into 3

3 cups frozen mixed berries, thawed and drained

CRUMBLE TOPPING

1 ½ cups plain flour

1 cup oats

¾ cup light brown sugar

¼ teaspoon ground cinnamon

¼ teaspoon salt

150 g Western Star Chef's Choice Cultured Unsalted Butter, cut into cubes

ORANGE CUSTARD

300 ml bottle Western Star Thickened Cream

1 orange, rind zested

2 egg yolks

¼ cup caster sugar

2 teaspoons cornflour

METHOD

APPLE-BERRY MIXTURE

1. In a medium (about 2 litre capacity) oven-proof frying pan, combine the butter and sugar. Cook over medium heat, stirring, until melted and combined. Add the apple and toss well to coat. Cover with the lid and simmer for 10 minutes, stirring occasionally. Toss through the mixed berries.

CRUMBLE TOPPING

2. Preheat oven to 200°C / 185°C fan-forced. Place the flour, oats, sugar, cinnamon and salt in a large bowl, and use your fingertips to rub the Butter into the dry ingredients until large clumps form. Scatter over the berry mixture to evenly coat.

3. Bake in oven for 30-35 minutes or until top is golden and juice is bubbling.

4. While the crumble is cooking, make the orange custard.

ORANGE CUSTARD

5. Pour the cream into a small saucepan over medium-low heat. Add almost all the orange zest (reserving a small amount to garnish) and stir to combine. Bring to just before boiling point and turn off heat.

6. Place the egg yolks, sugar and cornflour in a large heat-proof bowl. Use a balloon whisk to whisk until pale and creamy. Gradually pour the hot cream mixture into the egg yolk mixture, whisking constantly, until combined and smooth. Return to the saucepan over very low heat. Stir constantly for about 5 minutes or until custard is thickened and coats the back of a wooden spoon.

7. Serve the crumble with the orange custard and sprinkled with reserved orange zest.

DAIRY-FREE LEMON AVOCADO
pound cake

 PREP 15 MINS **COOK** 50 MINS 👤 **SERVES** 8

INGREDIENTS

AVOCADO CAKE

1¼ cups plain wholemeal flour

¼ cup cornflour

1 tablespoon baking powder

1 cup raw caster sugar

½ cup desiccated coconut

¼ cup coconut oil

2 eggs

2 teaspoons finely grated lemon rind

2 medium avocados, mashed
(1¼ cups mashed)

½ cup coconut milk

¼ cup shredded coconut

COCONUT ICING

400ml tin coconut cream

1½ tablespoons honey

METHOD

AVOCADO CAKE

1. Preheat oven to 180°C / 160°C fan-forced and line a loaf tin with baking paper.

2. Place the flour, cornflour, baking powder, sugar and coconut in a large bowl and mix together. Make a well in the centre and add the oil, eggs, lemon rind, avocado and coconut milk. Whisk until just combined.

3. Pour into loaf tin and bake for 50 minutes, or until a skewer inserted into the centre comes out clean. Allow to cool in tin completely.

4. Meanwhile, make the icing.

5. When ready to serve, spoon the icing over the cake and scatter with shredded coconut.

COCONUT ICING

6. Place the coconut cream in the fridge for 24 hours. Once chilled completely, remove the top firm creamy layer and place in a large bowl (you should have about ¾ cup).

TIPS & HINTS:

Coconut cream varies in consistency from brand to brand and after refrigeration, some coconut creams may be thicker than others. If your icing is very thick, add a few tablespoons of coconut milk or water to thin the icing.

Tip

Serve pudding with pouring cream or ice-cream.

CHESTNUT & GOLDEN SYRUP
pudding

 **PREP** 20 MINS **COOK** 50 MINS **SERVES** 4-6

INGREDIENTS

220g fresh chestnuts

½ cup milk

1 egg

80g butter, melted

2 tbsp golden syrup

⅓ cup firmly-packed brown sugar

1¼ cups self-raising flour, sifted

½ cup brown sugar

2 tsp cornflour

1¼ cups boiling water

¼ cup golden syrup

Icing sugar, for dusting

METHOD

1. Cut chestnuts in half across the width of the chestnut.

2. Place prepared chestnuts into a saucepan of cold water and bring to the boil.

3. Simmer for 15-20 minutes. Remove the chestnuts one at a time from the water.

4. Wrap in a clean tea towel for 5-10 minutes. While chestnuts are still warm, quickly peel off the outer brown shell and remove the papery thin skin underneath.

5. Preheat oven to 180°C / 160°C fan-forced. Lightly grease an 8-cup deep ovenproof dish.

6. Finely grate chestnuts in a food processor. In a large bowl, combine milk, egg, butter and golden syrup. Stir in chestnuts, sugar and sifted flour. Using a large metal spoon, mix until just combined. Spoon into the prepared dish.

7. To make the sauce, combine sugar and cornflour in a small bowl. Sprinkle over pudding. Combine water and golden syrup in a jug. Pour mixture over the back of large metal spoon over the pudding batter. Place dish on a baking tray lined with baking paper.

8. Bake for 50-55 minutes until golden and pudding bounces back when gently pressed in the centre. Stand for 5 minutes. Dust with icing sugar.

SLOW COOKED LAMB SHANK RAGU WITH PAPPARDELLE

PREP 10 MIN   COOK 3.5 HOURS   SERVES 6

INGREDIENTS

2 tbsp. olive oil

4 lamb shanks

1 (150 g) medium onion, diced

2 cups (500 ml) tomato and basil passata

1 cup (250 ml) beef stock

Salt and pepper to taste

1 tbsp. (20 g) butter

½ cup (45 g) Extra Sharp Parmesan, grated

400 g packet dried pappardelle

1 ¼ cups (90 g) Extra Sharp Parmesan, shaved

METHOD

1. Preheat oven to 160°C / 140°C fan-forced.

2. Heat half the oil in over medium-high heat in a large stovetop and ovenproof casserole dish. Brown the shanks all over then set aside.

3. Add remaining oil to pan and add onion, cook for 3-4 minutes. Stir in passata and stock and bring to the simmer. Return the lamb shanks back to the casserole dish and cover with lid and cook for approximately 3 hours or until the meat is falling off the bone.

4. Remove the shanks from the pan and shred the lamb with two forks. Return to casserole dish to warm through. Season with salt and pepper and stir in butter and grated Parmesan. Keep warm.

5. Meanwhile, cook the pasta in a large saucepan according to packet instructions. Drain well.

6. Add pasta to ragu and stir through to coat. Transfer to a serving dish and sprinkle with shaved Parmesan.

TIPS

This dish is ideal to make ahead. Reheat in slow cooker on low before adding pasta.

You can also cook this recipe in a slow cooker. Be sure to sear the shanks and cook the onion before adding to the slow cooker to enhance the flavours.

OVEN-BAKED CHICKEN & VEGETABLE RISOTTO

PREP 10 MIN   COOK 35 MIN   SERVES 4-6

INGREDIENTS

300 g frozen beans, broccoli and carrot mix

2 tbsp. olive oil

2 (500 g) chicken breast fillets, thickly sliced

1 brown onion, finely chopped

2 garlic cloves, crushed

1½ cup (300 g) Arborio rice

4 cups (1 L) salt-reduced chicken stock

½ cup frozen peas

25 g Western Star Original Salted Butter, chopped

1 cup (90 g) Extra Sharp Parmesan Grated

METHOD

1. Preheat the oven to 200°C / 180°C fan-forced. Remove frozen vegetables from freezer to thaw slightly.

2. Heat half the oil in a large flameproof, ovenproof dish over medium-high heat. Add the chicken and cook for 3 minutes or until golden brown. Remove from pan.

3. Heat remaining oil in dish. Add onion and garlic and cook, stirring, for 3-4 minutes or until softened. Add rice and cook, stirring, for 1 minute.

4. Add stock and bring to the boil. Cover. Transfer to oven. Bake for 15 minutes. Remove from oven. Stir in vegetable mix and peas. Bake, uncovered, for 10 minutes or until rice is tender and liquid absorbed.

5. Stir in butter and ¾ cup (70 g) of the Parmesan until melted and combined. Return chicken to the pan. Scatter with remaining Parmesan and return to oven to cook for 5 minutes or until cheese has melted.

PARMESAN CRUSTED CHICKEN DRUMSTICKS PARMIGIANA

PREP 15 MIN   COOK 35 MIN   SERVES 4

INGREDIENTS

2 eggs

1 ½ cups (135 g) panko breadcrumbs

1 cup (90 g) Parmesan Grated

Salt and pepper

8 medium chicken drumsticks, skin on

⅓ cup (80 ml) vegetable oil

700 g tomato passata with basil and oregano

2 ¼ cups (200 g) 4 Cheese Melt

METHOD

1. Preheat the oven to 200°C / 180°C fan-forced. Line a baking tray with baking paper.

2. Lightly whisk the eggs in a shallow dish with ¼ cup water.

3. In a large mixing bowl combine the panko breadcrumbs and Parmesan cheese and season well with salt and pepper.

4. Working with one drumstick at a time, dip in the egg, then breadcrumb mixture, pressing the crumbs on gently with your fingertips to coat. Set aside.

5. Heat half of the oil in a large frying pan, over medium-high heat. Cook half of the drumsticks for 3 minutes on each side, or until golden and crisp. Transfer to the lined tray and repeat with the remaining oil and chicken.

6. Meanwhile, spread the tomato passata over the base of a 6 cup (1.5 litre) capacity ovenproof dish. Arrange the drumsticks over the tomatoes and top with the 4 Cheese Melt.

7. Return to the oven and bake for 15-20 minutes, or until the cheese is melted and chicken is cooked and golden. Serve warm with a fresh salad.

BACON, BROCCOLI & PARMESAN PASTA

PREP 5 MIN
COOK 15 MIN
SERVES 4

INGREDIENTS

375 g casarecce pasta

2 tbsp. olive oil

4 rashers streaky rindless bacon, chopped

300 g broccoli, trimmed and coarsely chopped

2 cloves garlic, crushed

Salt and pepper to taste

1 ⅓ cups (125 g)
          Grated

METHOD

1. Bring a large pot of salted water to the boil and cook pasta according to packet instructions. Drain, reserving ⅓ cup of the cooking water.

2. Heat oil in a large heavy based pan over medium-high heat. Add bacon and cook, stirring frequently for 3 minutes or until browned.

3. Add broccoli and garlic and reduce heat to medium. Cook for a further 3 minutes or until broccoli has softened but still retains a bite.

4. Stir in cooked pasta and pasta water and toss to coat. Season with salt and pepper and stir through half the Parmesan. Serve immediately topped with remaining Parmesan.

CHICKEN, SPINACH & MUSHROOM LASAGNE

PREP 15 MIN   COOK 55 MIN   SERVES 8

INGREDIENTS

LASAGNE FILLING

2 tbsp. olive oil

1 (80 g) small onion, finely chopped

2 cloves garlic, crushed

1 kg chicken mince

200 g Swiss brown mushrooms, sliced

1 tbsp. plain flour

300 ml cooking cream

2 tbsp. Dijon mustard

Salt and pepper

375 g packet fresh lasagne sheets

120 g baby spinach leaves, roughly chopped

RICOTTA TOPPING

500 g Ricotta

1 egg, lightly beaten

½ cup (125 ml) milk

450 g Perfect Bakes cheese

METHOD

LASAGNE FILLING

1. Preheat oven to 200°C / 180°C fan-forced. Lightly grease an 8 cup (2 litre) ovenproof lasagne dish.
2. To make the filling, heat oil in a large frying pan over medium heat. Add onion and garlic. Cook, stirring for 1-2 minutes or until onion softens.
3. Add mince and cook for 2-3 minutes, breaking up the mince until browned. Add mushrooms and cook for 1 minute.
4. Stir through the flour and cook a further 1 minute. Add cooking cream and mustard and mix well. Reduce heat and simmer uncovered on low for 5 minutes or until sauce thickens. Season with salt and pepper and set aside.

RICOTTA TOPPING:

1. Mix together the Ricotta, eggs, and milk. Season with salt and pepper. Stir through ½ cup of the Perfect Bakes cheese. Refrigerate until ready to use. Reserve remaining cheese.

TO ASSEMBLE LASAGNE

1. Spread ⅓ cup of the ricotta topping over base of dish. Top with lasagne sheets, trimming to fit the size of the dish if necessary.
2. Stir chopped spinach through remaining Ricotta topping; divide into three portions.
3. Top lasagne sheet layer with one third of the chicken mix, sprinkle with a handful of Perfect Bakes cheese and cover with another layer of lasagne sheets. Continue layering with chicken mix, then Perfect Bakes cheese, followed by a layer of Ricotta and spinach sauce. Repeat these layers again, finishing with a layer of lasagne sheets.
4. Spread the remaining ricotta and spinach sauce over the top and sprinkle with remaining cheese. Bake uncovered for 35 – 40 minutes until golden and lasagne sheets are cooked. Stand 10 minutes before serving. Serve with fresh green salad.

QUICK CHICKEN, SPINACH & PUMPKIN PASTA BAKE

PREP 5 MIN   COOK 25 MIN   SERVES 6

INGREDIENTS

500 g dried rigatoni

1 tbsp. olive oil

500 g chicken mince

2 cloves garlic, crushed

500 g tinned pumpkin soup

120 g baby spinach leaves

3 ⅓ cups (300 g) Perfect Bakes cheese

METHOD

1. Preheat oven to 200°C / 180°C fan-forced.

2. Bring a large pot of salted water to the boil and cook rigatoni according to packet instructions. Drain and set aside.

3. Meanwhile, heat oil in a large pan over medium-high heat. Add chicken mince and garlic and cook, stirring frequently for 3 minutes breaking up chicken mince.

4. Stir through soup and reduce heat to low; simmer for 2 minutes uncovered. Add baby spinach leaves, stir to wilt. Add half of the Perfect Bakes cheese, mix through and then add cooked pasta stirring to ensure pasta is evenly covered.

5. Spoon pasta into an 8 cup (2 litre) capacity baking dish. Top with remaining Perfect Bakes cheese.

6. Bake in the oven for 15 minutes or until cheese is melted and golden. Serve hot with steamed seasonal vegetables.

CHEESY SWEET POTATO, POTATO & SAGE GRATIN

PREP 20 MIN   COOK 60 MIN   SERVES 6

INGREDIENTS

2 tsp. butter

3 cloves garlic

2 tbsp. fresh sage

1.2 kg Sebago potatoes, peeled and cut into 5 mm thick slices

900 g sweet potato, peeled and cut into 5 mm thick slices

Salt and black pepper, to taste

300 ml cream

2 ¼ cups (200 g) Perfect Bakes cheese

METHOD

1. Preheat oven to 200°C / 180°C fan-forced.

2. Grease an 8 cup (2 litre) capacity baking dish with the butter.

3. Finely chop garlic and sage together.

4. Arrange a layer of white potato slices onto the base of the dish, overlapping slightly. Season with salt and pepper and sprinkle with a small amount of the chopped garlic, sage and cream. Add 2 tbsp. of the Perfect Bakes cheese over the potatoes.

5. Next, top with a layer of sweet potato slices and continue layering with the garlic, sage, cream and cheese. Repeat layers of white potato and sweet potato until all of the vegetables have been used.

6. Top the final layer with remaining cheese and season again with salt and pepper.

7. Bake 55-60 minutes or until potatoes are cooked and top is golden. Stand for 5-10 minutes before serving.

QUICK SAUSAGE PASTA BAKE

PREP 10 MIN   COOK 20 MIN   SERVES 4

INGREDIENTS

375 g dried casarecce pasta

1 tbsp. olive oil

500 g Italian-style pork and fennel sausages, casing removed

200 g Swiss brown mushrooms, quartered

¼ - ½ tsp. dried chilli flakes

2 x 420 g jars tomato-based pasta sauce

1⅔ cups (150 g) Perfect Bakes cheese

Salt and pepper, to taste

60 g baby rocket leaves

200 g grape tomatoes, sliced

METHOD

1. Preheat grill to high. Cook pasta in large saucepan of boiling water, until just tender; drain. Return to pan.

2. Meanwhile, heat oil in a large deep-frying pan over medium-high heat. Add sausage mince to pan and cook, breaking up with a wooden spoon, for 5 minutes or until browned. Add mushrooms and chilli. Cook, stirring, for 5 minutes or until just tender.

3. Add sauce. Stir to coat. Bring to the boil. Add pasta. Simmer, for 2 minutes or until warmed through and pasta is coated in sauce. Season with salt and pepper. Transfer to a baking dish. Top with Perfect Bakes cheese. Grill pasta bake for 4-5 minutes or until cheese is golden and melted.

4. Top with half the rocket and tomatoes and serve pasta bake with remaining salad on the side.

TIP

You can use a flameproof baking dish or ovenproof frying pan in this recipe. This way you can just top with cheese and transfer straight to oven!

CHICKEN & RICE ENCHILADAS

PREP 10 MIN   COOK 25 MIN   SERVES 4

INGREDIENTS

1 x 375 g jar mild tomato salsa

2 tbsp. olive oil

500 g chicken mince

1 x 30 g sachet taco spice mix

1 x 250 g packet microwave brown rice, cooked

1 x 400 g can black beans, rinsed, drained

2 spring onions, finely sliced

1 ⅔ cups (150 g) 4 Cheese Melt

1 x 400 g packet (10) regular flour tortillas

1 x 400 g can diced tomatoes

1 avocado, diced

5 red cherry tomatoes, quartered

5 yellow grape tomatoes, quartered

Coriander leaves, to serve

METHOD

1. Preheat oven to 200°C / 180°C fan-forced. Grease a 12 cup (3 litre) capacity rectangular ovenproof dish. Spread ⅓ cup of the tomato salsa over base of prepared dish.

2. Heat oil in a large non-stick frypan over medium-high heat. Add chicken mince and cook, stirring to break up lumps for 5 minutes or until browned. Add taco spice mix and stir to combine. Add rice, beans, spring onion and 2 tbsp. of remaining salsa. Stir to combine.

3. For each enchilada, place a tortilla on a flat work surface. Top with 2 heaped tbsp. of chicken mixture and a tbsp. of 4 Cheese Melt. Roll up to enclose filling and form a log. Place, seam-side down in prepared dish. Repeat to make 10 enchiladas in total.

4. Whisk remaining salsa and diced tomato in a jug. Pour tomato mixture over top of enchiladas and sprinkle with remaining cheese. Bake for 25 minutes or until golden brown. Remove from oven. Stand for 5 minutes.

5. Serve enchiladas topped with avocado, tomatoes and coriander leaves.

IMPOSSIBLE PASTA PIE

PREP 10 MIN COOK 35 MIN SERVES 6

INGREDIENTS

1 ½ cups (250 g) macaroni

2 tbsp. chopped fresh oregano

2 cups (400 g) leftover roast vegetables, (roast pumpkin, onion, carrot, sweet potato), diced

⅓ cup (50 g) frozen peas

Salt and pepper

4 eggs

¾ cup (185 ml) milk

2 ¼ cups (200 g) 4 Cheese Melt

METHOD

1. Preheat oven to 200°C / 180°C fan-forced. Grease a 23 cm pie dish.

2. Cook pasta in a large saucepan according to packet instructions. Drain and set aside.

3. Combine the cooked macaroni with oregano, leftover vegetables and peas and season to taste with salt and pepper.

4. Whisk together the eggs and milk; add 4 Cheese Melt and mix well. Pour over the pasta and toss to coat. Spoon into the prepared pie dish and place on a baking tray in the oven.

5. Bake for 20 minutes uncovered, or until the pie is golden on the top, cover with foil and bake a further 5 minutes until set.

6. Remove the foil and allow the pie to sit for 10 minutes before cutting into wedges. Serve warm.

TIPS

Use any leftover baked vegetables, or substitute with frozen mixed vegetables.

At the end of the cooking time, press the pie gently in the middle; if it easily springs back, your pie is completely cooked. Otherwise, return to the oven covered with the foil for a further 5 minutes.

FAST FAMILY CHICKEN PIE

PREP 5 MIN COOK 30 MIN SERVES 6

INGREDIENTS

220 g frozen shortcrust pastry pie case

4 eggs

⅓ cup (80 ml) thickened cream

2 green onions, finely sliced

1 tbsp. chopped parsley (optional)

1 ⅔ cups (150 g) 4 Cheese Melt

150 g chopped or shredded cold BBQ chicken

METHOD

1. Arrange oven shelf to the lower middle position in the oven. Preheat oven 200°C / 180°C fan-forced.

2. Place pastry case onto a metal baking tray and bake for 5 minutes; remove and set aside.

3. Whisk together eggs, cream, green onions, parsley and ¾ of the 4 Cheese Melt and mix well. Stir though chopped chicken.

4. Carefully pour mixture into pastry case and smooth the surface. Top with remaining cheese.

5. Bake 20-25 minutes or until pastry is golden and eggs are set. Cheese should be melted and golden brown. Remove and stand 5 minutes.

6. Cut into wedges and serve with green salad.

TIPS

Ready-made shortcrust pastry cases are available from the freezer section at most supermarkets.

Serve with fresh side salad of garden peas, black olives, salad leaves and shaved Parmesan.

EASY FAMILY SHEPHERD'S PIE WITH CHEESY MASH

PREP 15 MIN   COOK 35 MIN   SERVES 6

INGREDIENTS

CHEESY MASH

1.2 kg white, floury potatoes, peeled and cut into 2.5 cm dice

30 g butter, diced

⅓ cup (80 ml) milk

2 ¼ cups (200 g) 4 Cheese Melt

LAMB FILLING

2 tbsp. olive oil

1 (150 g) onion, finely chopped

1 (120 g) carrot, finely diced

2 cloves garlic, crushed

500 g lamb mince

1 tbsp. plain flour

1 tbsp. tomato paste

1 cup (250 ml) beef stock

2 tbsp. Worcestershire sauce

1 cup (120 g) frozen peas

METHOD

CHEESY MASH

1. Place potatoes into a large pan and just cover with cold water. Bring to the boil and cook 20 minutes or until tender. Drain and return potato to warm pan to dry out slightly.

2. Mash until smooth and add butter, milk and half the 4 Cheese Melt. Mix well until smooth and creamy.

LAMB FILLING

1. Meanwhile, preheat oven to 200°C / 180°C fan-forced.

2. Heat oil in a large non-stick frying pan over medium-high heat and add onion. Cook for 3 minutes. Add carrot, garlic and mince and cook, stirring and breaking up meat until vegetables have softened and mince is browned.

3. Stir in flour and cook for 1 minute. Add tomato paste, stock and Worcestershire sauce. Bring sauce to the simmer and cook for 10 minutes or until sauce has thickened. Stir through peas.

4. Spoon into a large 8 cup (2 litre) baking dish. Top with mash and sprinkle with remaining cheese. Bake 10-15 minutes or until mash is golden. Let the pie sit for 10 minutes to set before serving.

TIPS

Use floury potatoes such as brushed or Sebago potatoes.

MONKEY BREAD 3 WAYS

PREP 15 MINS + PROVING TIME

INGREDIENTS

BASIC PIZZA DOUGH

2 tsp. (7 g sachet) dried yeast

1 cup (250 ml) lukewarm water

2 ⅔ cups (400 g) plain flour, plus extra to dust

2 tsp. salt

3 tbsp. olive oil

METHOD

BASIC PIZZA DOUGH

1. Add yeast to warm water and mix well. Stand for a few minutes until bubbles form on the surface of the water

2. Place flour and salt into a large mixing bowl. Make a well in the centre. Pour in the yeast mixture along with the oil.

3. Using your hands, mix the dough until it comes together into a ball and is smooth.

4. Turn out onto a lightly floured work surface and knead for a few minutes.

5. Place dough in a lightly oiled bowl and cover with cling wrap. Set aside in a warm place to rise for 30 minutes or until it doubles in size.

6. Turn dough out onto a lightly floured work surface and knead gently for 5 minutes or until smooth.

TIPS

For recipes that require only ½ quantity basic pizza dough, flatten out remaining pizza dough to form a disc. Wrap in cling film and place into a sealed container. Label and freeze for up to two months.

Defrost dough in refrigerator overnight.

CHEESE & CHIVE MONKEY BREAD

PREP 15 MINS + PROVING TIME
COOK 15 MIN
SERVES 4

INGREDIENTS

Cooking spray

½ quantity basic pizza dough (see page 33)

1 ⅔ (150 g)
Perfect Pizza cheese

2 tsp. garlic salt

¼ cup finely chopped chives

METHOD

1. Preheat oven to 200°C / 180°C fan-forced. Spray a 20 cm round cake pan or ovenproof frypan with oil.

2. Flatten dough out to form a 20 cm disc. Add ½ cup of the Perfect Pizza cheese, garlic salt and 2 tbsp. of the chives. Fold over dough and knead for about 3 minutes or until cheese and herbs are combined and evenly mixed in.

3. Shape dough into 3 cm thick log. Cut into 14 portions and roll into even sized balls. Place, side by side over base of prepared pan.

4. Bake for 10 minutes then remove pan and sprinkle over remaining cheese. Lightly spray with cooking spray then return to oven and bake for a further 5-10 minutes or until cheese is golden brown and melted.

5. Serve warm topped with remaining chives.

HAWAIIAN HAM & PINEAPPLE MONKEY BREAD

PREP 15 MINS + PROVING TIME
COOK 15 MIN
SERVES 6-8

INGREDIENTS

1 quantity basic pizza dough (see page 33)

2 ¼ cups (200 g)   **Perfect Pizza cheese**

150 g ham, finely diced

⅓ cup (80 g) drained canned pineapple chunks, finely diced

1 tbsp. pizza sauce

METHOD

1. Preheat oven to 200°C / 180°C fan-forced and line a baking tray with baking paper.

2. Turn dough out onto a lightly floured work surface and knead gently for 5 minutes or until smooth.

3. Roll dough to form a 20 cm disc. Add one cup of Perfect Pizza cheese and half the ham and pineapple. Fold over and knead until combined and evenly mixed.

4. Cut dough in half and roll each piece into 3 cm thick logs. Divide each dough log into 12 pieces. Roll into balls and position on baking tray in a spiral shape starting with one ball in the middle and building out around it.

5. Cover loosely with a clean tea towel and stand in a warm place for 30 minutes or until doubled in size.

6. Brush over pizza sauce and scatter over remaining ham and pineapple pieces.

7. Bake for 15 minutes, then remove and sprinkle with remaining cheese. Bake for a further 10 minutes or until cheese is melted and bread is cooked. Stand on tray for 5 minutes before serving.

GARLIC & HERB MONKEY BREAD WITH HOT CHEESY DIP

PREP 25 MINS + PROVING TIME
COOK 20 MIN
SERVES 6-8

INGREDIENTS

GARLIC BUTTER

80 g softened butter

½ tsp. garlic salt

1 small clove garlic, crushed

½ tsp. dried Italian herbs

MONKEY BREAD

1 quantity basic pizza dough
(see page 33)

**2 ¼ (200 g)
Perfect Pizza cheese**

1 tbsp. pesto

HOT CHEESY DIP

250 g cream cheese, softened
and diced

⅓ cup sour cream

2 green onions, finely chopped

**¼ cup (25g) Perfect Italiano™
Parmesan, Grated**

GARLIC & HERB MONKEY BREAD WITH HOT CHEESY DIP

METHOD

GARLIC BUTTER

1. Combine butter, garlic salt, garlic and dried herbs and mix well. Refrigerate until firm and cold reserving one tbsp. for the Cheesy Dip.

MONKEY BREAD

1. Preheat oven 200°C / 180°C fan-forced.

2. Place a one cup (250 ml) ovenproof ramekin into the centre of a piece of baking paper. Draw around the base. Turn paper over and place onto a large flat baking tray.

3. Roll out dough to form a 20 cm disc. Add ½ cup Perfect Pizza cheese, fold over and knead until combined and evenly mixed.

4. Cut dough in half and roll each piece into 3 cm thick logs. Divide each into 12 pieces and roll into balls.

5. Take a ½ tsp. of the cold garlic butter and push into the centre of a dough ball. Reroll to enclose. Repeat with remaining butter and dough.

6. Position stuffed dough balls around the drawn circle and form two rows. Cover with a clean tea towel and stand in a warm place for 15 minutes until risen slightly. When ready to cook, brush with pesto.

7. Bake for 10 minutes and while cooking, make the Cheesy Dip.

8. Remove the tray and place ramekin filled with Cheesy Dip into the centre of the Monkey Bread. Sprinkle remaining cheese over the rolls. Return to oven and cook a further 5-10 minutes or until cheese has melted and golden. Transfer to a serving tray and serve immediately.

CHEESY DIP

1. Place one tbsp. of the prepared garlic butter mixture, cream cheese and sour cream into a small saucepan. Stir over low heat until hot and smooth. Stir through green onion and Parmesan cheese. Spoon into reserved ramekin.

30 MINUTE PIZZA PASTA BAKE

PREP 10 MIN   COOK 20 MIN   SERVES 4-6

INGREDIENTS

500 g potato gnocchi or dried orecchiette pasta

100 g sliced pepperoni

1 tbsp. olive oil

1 red onion, thinly sliced

100 g button mushrooms, sliced

1 green capsicum, thinly sliced

1 x 400 g can crushed tomatoes with basil and oregano

Salt and pepper, to taste

1⅔ cups (150 g)   Perfect Pizza cheese

¼ tsp. dried oregano

¼ tsp. dried chilli flakes (optional)

Fresh oregano leaves, to serve

METHOD

1. Cook gnocchi in large saucepan of boiling water, until just tender, following the packet instructions.

2. Meanwhile, reserve 8 pepperoni slices. Cut the remaining pepperoni slices into quarters.

3. Heat oil in an ovenproof frying pan over medium-high heat. Add onion, mushroom, capsicum and quartered pepperoni. Cook, stirring occasionally, for 5-7 minutes or until vegetables are tender.

4. Add crushed tomato. Bring to the boil. Reduce heat and simmer, stirring occasionally, for 5-7 minutes or until mixture thickens. Season with salt and pepper. Stir in gnocchi. Level top.

5. Preheat grill on high. Sprinkle gnocchi with Perfect Pizza cheese. Top with reserved pepperoni, dried oregano and chilli flakes, if you like. Grill for 4-5 minutes or until cheese is golden. Sprinkle with fresh oregano to serve.

PERFECT PIE MAKER PIZZAS

PREP 25 MIN   COOK 15 MIN   MAKES 12 PIE MAKER PIZZAS

INGREDIENTS

PIZZA DOUGH

2 tsp. (7 g sachet) dried yeast

1 cup (250 ml) lukewarm water

2 ⅔ cups (400 g) plain flour, plus extra to dust

2 tsp. salt

3 tbsp. olive oil

PROSCIUTTO AND BLACK OLIVE PIE MAKER PIZZA

½ quantity of pizza dough

½ cup pizza sauce

1 ⅔ cups (150 g)

Perfect Pizza cheese

50 g prosciutto, torn

2 tbsp. sliced pitted black olives

HAWAIIAN PIE MAKER PIZZA

½ quantity of pizza dough

½ cup pizza sauce

1 ⅔ cups (150 g)

Perfect Pizza cheese

⅓ cup diced ham

1 cup drained and diced pineapple pieces

PERFECT PIE MAKER PIZZAS

METHOD

PIZZA DOUGH

1. Add yeast to warm water and mix well. Stand for a few minutes until bubbles form on the surface of the water

2. Place flour and salt into a large mixing bowl. Make a well in the centre. Pour in the yeast mixture along with the oil.

3. Using your hands, mix the dough until it comes together into a ball and is smooth.

4. Turn out onto a lightly floured work surface and knead for a few minutes.

5. Place dough in a lightly oiled bowl and cover with cling wrap. Set aside in a warm place to rise for 30 minutes or until it doubles in size.

6. Turn dough out onto a lightly floured work surface and knead gently for 5 minutes or until smooth.

7. Roll out pizza dough on a lightly floured surface to 5mm thick. Using the lid cutter of the pie maker cut 12 rounds.

8. Lightly grease the pie holes in the piemaker and follow manufacturer's instructions to preheat.

PROSCIUTTO AND BLACK OLIVE PIE MAKER PIZZA

1. Place one dough round into each of the holes, top with two tsp. of the pizza sauce, a sprinkling of Perfect Pizza cheese.

2. Add prosciutto and black olives and top with more cheese .

3. Close lid of pie maker and cook for about 5 minutes, or until the pizza base is cooked, and the top golden. Repeat with remaining dough, cheese and pizza toppings.

4. Serve while warm.

HAWAIIAN PIE MAKER PIZZA

1. Place one dough round into each of the holes, top with two tsp. of the pizza sauce, a sprinkling of Perfect Pizza cheese.

2. Add ham and pineapple and top with more cheese.

3. Close lid of pie maker and cook for about 5 minutes, or until the pizza base is cooked, and the top golden. Repeat with remaining dough, cheese and pizza toppings

4. Serve while warm.

TIP

These pizzas are an ideal lunch box filler. Once cooked, cool and wrap individually or pack 2 or 3 into containers. Freeze for up to one month. For lunch box, defrost in fridge overnight. Or reheat in pie maker for 3 minutes.

FREEZER TIP

Flatten out remaining pizza dough to form a disc. Wrap in cling film and place into a sealed container. Label and freeze for up to two months.

Defrost in the refrigerator overnight.

FAMILY SAUSAGE ROLL WITH MOZZARELLA

PREP 15 MIN   COOK 55 MIN   SERVES 6

INGREDIENTS

SAUSAGE ROLL

750 g beef mince

1 cup (90 g) soft fresh breadcrumbs

1 egg, lightly whisked, plus 1 extra

1 carrot, finely grated

1 clove garlic, crushed

⅓ cup (35 g) Parmesan Grated

2 sheets frozen puff pastry, thawed

¼ cup Perfect Basil Pesto (see recipe, below)

2½ cups (225 g) Mozzarella

PERFECT BASIL PESTO

⅓ cup pine nuts, toasted

3 cups basil leaves

1 garlic clove, roughly chopped

⅔ cup (70 g) Parmesan Grated

⅔ cup (165 ml) olive oil

METHOD

SAUSAGE ROLL

1. Preheat oven to 220°C / 200°C fan-forced. Grease and line a large oven tray with baking paper.

2. Combine the mince, breadcrumbs, egg, carrot, garlic and 2 tbsp. Parmesan in a bowl. Mix well.

3. Place pastry sheets side by side on a clean work surface. Join edges together using finger tips or lightly press with a rolling pin to form one large long pastry sheet. Spoon mince mixture along centre of pastry, and flatten to cover pastry, leaving a 2 cm border. Spoon the pesto over the mince and spread out evenly.

4. Top mince with Mozzarella, piling together along centre to form a mound. Using pastry as a guide, roll mince tightly to form a log. Transfer, seam-side down to prepared tray. Score top every 4 cm. Brush pastry with extra egg and sprinkle with the remaining 2 tbsp. Parmesan.

5. Bake for 55 minutes or until golden brown and puffed. Remove from oven. Stand for 5 minutes before cutting to serve.

PERFECT BASIL PESTO

1. Note: If making pesto from scratch, allow extra 10 minutes to make this recipe which makes approximately one cup.

2. Place the pine nuts, basil, garlic, Parmesan and olive oil in a small food processor and whizz until finely chopped.

TIP

Pesto will keep for 2-3 days in a sterilised jar in the fridge. Be sure to add an extra 1-2cm of olive oil to cover the surface – this helps prevent pesto from oxidising and going brown.

30 MINUTE CHEESY CHICKEN RISONI

PREP 5 MIN COOK 25 MIN SERVES 4

INGREDIENTS

1 tbsp. olive oil

4 large chicken thighs, fat trimmed

1 (150 g) medium onion, diced

2 cloves garlic crushed

1 ½ cups (375 ml) tomato passata

1 ½ cups (375 ml) chicken stock

3 tbsp. chopped fresh oregano

¾ cup (170g) risoni

1 ⅔ cups (150 g)

Grated Mozzarella

METHOD

1. Preheat the oven to 200°C / 180°C fan-forced.

2. Heat the oil in an ovenproof pan, over medium-high heat. Add chicken and cook for 1-2 minutes on each side, until golden brown. Remove the chicken from the pan and set aside.

3. Add onion and garlic and cook 2-3 minutes or until the onion has softened. Stir in passata and stock, reduce heat and bring to a simmer. Add oregano, stir through the risoni then place the cooked chicken thighs over the top. Cover with a lid or foil and bake in the oven for 10 minutes.

4. Remove lid and sprinkle Mozzarella over the chicken. Return to the oven with the lid off and bake a further 10 minutes, or until cheese has melted and golden. Serve immediately.

MOZZARELLA TORTELLINI

PREP 5 MIN
COOK 25 MIN
SERVES 4

INGREDIENTS

2 tbsp. olive oil

1 small onion, finely diced

4 cloves garlic, crushed

750 ml tomato passata

Salt and pepper

½ cup coarsely chopped fresh basil leaves, plus extra for garnish

625 g fresh spinach & ricotta tortellini

1 ⅔ cups (150 g)
Grated Mozzarella

METHOD

1. Heat oil in a large frying pan over medium-high heat. Add onion and garlic and cook, stirring frequently for 3 minutes or until softened.

2. Add passata and 1 cup water; bring to the boil. Reduce heat to medium and simmer for 10 minutes. Stir through basil, season to taste. Add tortellini and continue to cook for 3 minutes or until pasta is tender.

3. Top with Mozzarella and brown under a preheated grill for 5 minutes or until cheese is golden and melted. Top with extra basil leaves then serve immediately with green salad.

TIP

Use any fresh filled pasta available at the supermarket.

SPINACH & RICOTTA CANNELLONI

PREP 15 MIN   COOK 30 MIN   SERVES 4

INGREDIENTS

1 tbsp. olive oil, plus extra for drizzling

2 tbsps. (40 g) Western Star Original Butter

2 cloves garlic, finely chopped

¼ tsp. ground nutmeg

150 g baby spinach, washed and finely chopped

500 g tub
   Ricotta

½ cup (50 g)
   Parmesan
Grated

16 cannelloni tubes

1 x 700 ml bottle passata

2 ¼ cups (200 g)
   Mozzarella

Mixed green salad, to serve

METHOD

1. Preheat oven to 180°C / 160°C fan-forced.

2. In a large non-stick frypan, heat the oil and butter. Add garlic and cook for a few minutes. Add nutmeg and spinach and cook for 5 minutes. Place in a bowl and set aside to cool.

3. Once spinach mixture is cool, add in Ricotta and ¼ cup of Parmesan, mixing well to combine. Using a piping bag squeeze the ricotta mixture into the cannelloni tubes.

4. Pour half the passata into a large baking dish. Layer the filled cannelloni on top, then spoon over the remaining passata. Drizzle with extra olive oil, then sprinkle the Mozzarella and remaining ¼ cup of Parmesan over the top. Bake for 25 minutes or until golden and bubbling.

5. Remove from oven and allow to cool for 5 minutes before serving with a green salad.

CPSIA information can be obtained
at www.ICGtesting.com
Printed in the USA
BVHW092254280421
605945BV00014B/1413

9 786154 476991